FLORIDA STATE
UNIVERSITY LIBRARIES

DEC 8 2006

Tallahassee Florida

The Besterman World Bibliographies

The Besterman World Bibliographies

Family History

A BIBLIOGRAPHY OF
BIBLIOGRAPHIES

By Theodore Besterman

TOTOWA, N. J.
Rowman and Littlefield
1971

Published by
Rowman and Littlefield
A Division of
Littlefield, Adams & Co.
81 Adams Drive
Totowa, N. J. 07512

★

Copyright © 1939, 1947, 1965, 1971
by Theodore Besterman
Printed in the United States of America

★

Typography by George Hornby
and Theodore Besterman

ISBN 0-87471-048-0

Contents

Family History, Genealogy, Heraldry	1
Names	55
Family Names	60
Place Names	110

Preface

I have explained in the Introduction to the successive editions of *A World bibliography of bibliographies* why I decided to arrange it alphabetically by specific subjects. Since that decision was taken, and after prolonged experience of the book in use, I have had no reason to regret it, nor among the many letters I have received from librarians has there been a single one complaining of the alphabetical form of the *World bibliography*.

The *World bibliography of bibliographies* covers all subjects and all languages, and is intended to serve reference and research purposes of the most specific and specialised kind. Yet contained in it are broad and detailed surveys which, if relevant entries throughout the volumes are added to them, can serve also the widest reference inquiries, and be useful to those who seek primary signposts to information in varied fields of inquiry.

Therefore I can only thank Rowman and Littlefield for having gathered together all the titles in some of the major fields found throughout the 6664 columns of the fourth edition (1965-1966) of *A World bibliography of bibliographies*.

Preface

These fields are:
1. Bibliography
2. Printing
3. Periodical Publications
4. Academic Writings
5. Art and Architecture
6. Music and Drama
7. Education
8. Agriculture
9. Medicine
10. Law
11. English and American Literature
12. Technology
13. Physical Sciences
14. Biological Sciences
15. Family History
16. Commerce, Manufactures, Labour
17. History
18. Geography

Of course these categories by no means exhaust the 117,000 separately collated volumes set out in the *World bibliography*, and the above titles will be added to if librarians wish for it.

Th. B.

Notes on the Arrangement

An Alternative to critical annotation

Consider what it is we look for in a normal bibliography of a special subject. Reflection will show, I think, that we look, above all, for completeness, just as we do in a bibliography of bibliographies. We desire completeness even more than accuracy (painfully uncongenial though it is for me to make such a statement); for in most cases a bibliography is intended to give us particulars of publications to which we wish to refer; thus we can always judge for ourselves (waiving gross errors) whether the bibliographer has correctly described these publications. On the other hand, anything that is omitted is lost until rediscovered.

The question is, therefore, whether it is possible to give some indication of the degree of completeness of a bibliography without indulging in the annotation which is impossible in a work of the present scope and scale. It seemed to me that this could be achieved, to a considerable extent, by

Notes

recording the approximate number of entries set out in it. This method is, of course, a rough-and-ready one, but experience shows that it is remarkably effective: and I hope that its novelty will not tell against it.

The recording of the number of works set out in a bibliography has another advantage in the case of serial publications: it displays in statistical form the development of the subject from year to year—often in a highly significant manner.

This procedure, then, is that which I have adopted, the number of items in each bibliography being shown in square brackets at the end of the entry. This, I may add, is by no means an easy or mechanical task, as can be judged from the fact that this process, on the average, just about doubles the time taken in entering each bibliography.

Supplementary information in footnotes

I have said that this method of indicating the number of entries is intended to replace critical treatment; but it is not possible to exclude annotation altogether, for a certain minimum of added information is indispensable. Consequently many of my entries will be seen to have footnotes, in which the following types of information are recorded: a few words of explanation where the title is inaccurate, misleading, obscure, or in-

Notes

sufficiently informative; a statement to that effect where a work is in progress, where intermediate volumes in a series have not been published, or where no more have been published; an attempt to clarify complicated series; a note that a book was privately printed or in a limited number of copies, where this does not exceed 500, or in some abnormal manner, as on one side of the leaf, on coloured paper, or in a reproduction of handwriting, or with erratic pagination; when I have come across copies containing manuscript or other added matter, I have recorded the fact; substantial corrections and additions to bibliographies are sometimes published in periodicals, and I have noted a good many of these—but without aiming at anything even remotely approaching completeness, the attainment of which would be impossible. Various minor types of information are also occasionally to be found in the footnotes.

Owing to the great increase in the number of bibliographies reproduced directly from typewritten copy, such publications are designated by an asterisk at the end of the entry; this device saves a good deal of space.

Place of publication

The place of publication is not shown when it is London in the case of an english book and

Notes

Paris in the case of a french one. In the case of a series or sequence of entries, however, the absence of a place of publication means that it is the same as the place last shown in the series. The same applies to the names of editors and compilers. The place of publication is given as it appears on the titlepage, but prepositions are omitted even if violence is done to grammatical construction.

The Order of entries

Under each heading the order of the entries is chronological by date of publication; in the case of works in successive volumes or editions the chronological order applies to the first volume or edition. In suitable long headings an additional chronological order by period covered has been created; see, for instance, France: History, or Drama: Great Britain.

Method of collating

An effort has been made, so far as space allows, to give detailed and accurate information of the kind more usually found in small bibliographies. For instance, I have paid special attention to the collation of bibliographies in several (or even numerous) parts or volumes. It is, in fact, difficult to understand why it is usually considered necessary to give collations of works in a single volume,

Notes

where difficulties seldom occur (from the point of view of systematic bibliography), but not of a work in several volumes, where confusion much more frequently arises. An occasional gap in the collations of such publications will be noticed. This is because, naturally enough, I have not been able in every case to see perfect sets; and I have thought it better to leave a very small number of such blanks rather than to hold up the bibliography indefinitely.

Serial publications

Where successive issues of a serial publication are set out, the year or period shown is usually that covered by the relevant issue; in such cases no date of publication is given unless publication was abnormal or erratic in relation to the period covered.

Bibliographies in more than one edition

Where a bibliography has gone into more than one edition I have tried (though I have not always been able) to record at least the first and latest editions. Intermediate editions have also been recorded wherever it seemed useful to do so, that is, for bibliographies first published before 1800, and for those of special interest or importance; but in general intermediate editions, though examined, have not been recorded.

Notes

Transcription of titles

Titles have been set out in the shortest possible form consistent with intelligibility and an adequate indication of the scope of the bibliography; omissions have of course been indicated. The author's name, generally speaking, is given as it appears on the titlepage, amplified and interpreted within square brackets where necessary.

Anonymous bibliographies

Far too large a proportion of bibliographical work is published anonymously. This is due, in part, to the all too common practice of library committees and similar bodies of suppressing altogether or of hiding in prefaces the names of those who have compiled bibliographies and catalogues for them. I have spent a good deal of time in excavating such and other evidences of authorship, and the result may be seen in the large number of titles preceded by names enclosed within square brackets.

Th. B.

Family history, genealogy, heraldry.

1. Periodicals, 2.
2. General, 2.
3. Countries.
   Austria, 9.
   Belgium, 10.
   Brazil, 10.
   Cuba, 10.
   Denmark, 10.
   Flanders, 11.
   France, 11.
   Germany, 14.
   Great Britain.
      a. General, 17.
      b. Inquisitiones post mortem, 22.
      c. Marriage licences, 25.
      d. Parish registers, 26.
      e. Visitations and pedigrees, 29.
      f. Wills and administrations, 31.
   Hungary, 35.

Family History

Ireland, 35.
Italy, 37.
Jews, 38.
Mauritius, 38.
Netherlands, 38.
Norway, 41.
Poland, 41.
Portugal, 41.
Prussia, 42.
Russia, 42.
Scotland, 43.
Spain, 46.
Sweden, 49.
Switzerland, 49.
United States, 50.

1. *Periodicals*

RICHARD ROSE, Familiengeschichtliche bibliographie. Heft 1. Allgemeine familiengeschichtliche zeitschriften. Von familien herausgegebene zeitschriften und familientagsberichte. Berlin 1917. pp.viii.64. [225.]
no more published.

2. *General*

THOMAS GORE, Catalogus, alphabeticè digestus, plerorumque omnium authorum, (tam antiquorum quàm recentiorum) qui de re heraldica latinè, gallicè, italicè, hispanicè, germanicè, anglicè, scripserunt. Oxon. 1668. pp.[viii].27. [200.]

—— [another edition]. 1674. pp.[xxx].139. [750.]

JACOB FRIEDRICH REIMMANN, Historia literaria de fatis studii genealogici apud Hebræos, Græcos, Romanos & Germanos, in qva scriptores harum gentium potissimi enumerantur. Ascan. &c. 1702. pp.[iv].120. [100.]

CAROLUS ARNDIUS, Bibliotheca politico-heraldica selecta, h.e. recensus scriptorum ad politicam atque heraldicam pertinentium. Rostochii &c. 1705. pp.[iii].552. [2500.]

JACOB FRIEDRICH REIMMANN, Historiæ literariæ exotericæ & acroamaticæ particula sive de libris genealogicis vulgatioribus & rarioribus commentatio. Lipsiæ &c. [1710]. pp.[ii].55.118.[xvii].20. [xvii]. [300.]

JOHANN HÜBNER, Bibliotheca genealogica, das ist: ein verzeichnis aller alten und neuen genealogischen bücher von allen nationen in der welt. Hamburg 1729. pp.[xiv].594.[xiv]. [750.]

Family History

CHRISTIAN SAM[UEL] THEODOR BERND, Allgemeine schriftenkunde der gesammten wappenwissenschaft. Bonn 1830–1841. pp.xxxii.364+vi.365–680+xviii.306+viii.120. [6000.]

[FÉLIX VICTOR GOETHALS and JULES FRANÇOIS CHARLES MARIE GHISLAIN HUYTTENS], Indicateur nobiliaire de France, de Belgique, de Hollande, d'Allemagne, d'Espagne, d'Italie et d'Angleterre, d'après les collections manuscrites des bibliothèques publiques de Belgique. 1869. pp.vii.638. [25,000.]

CATALOGUE of heraldic, genealogical, and antiquarian books and manuscripts, which belonged to the late Alexander Sinclair. Edinburgh 1877. pp.23. [500.]

privately printed; the collection was bequeathed to the earl of Glasgow.

ALEXANDRE PINCHART, Catalogue de la bibliothèque de m. F[élix] V[ictor] Goethals. Manuscrits. Bruxelles 1878. pp.468. [10,000.]

CATALOGUE des livres et manuscrits composant la bibliothèque héraldique et généalogique de m. Ernest de Rozière. [c.1880]. pp.[iii].321. [1935.]

A LIST of works on heraldry, or containing heraldic illustrations, in the National art library.

Family History

South Kensington museum: 1880. pp.32. [450.]
—— [second edition]. Heraldry. Victoria and Albert Museum: Classed catalogue of printed books: 1901. pp.viii.186. [2500.]

[P. A. VAN DEN VELDEN], Bibliographisch overzigt van belangrijke werken en geschriften over geschied-, oudheid-, geslacht-, wapen- en zegelkunde, in het jaar 1881 in druk verschenen. Vereeniging 'De nederlandsche heraut': 's-Gravenhage 1883. pp.57. [450.]

O. GUNDLACH, Bibliotheca familiarum nobilium. Repertorium gedruckter familien-geschichten und familien-nachrichten. Neubrandenburg 1883. pp. 260. [3500.]
—— Dritte ... auflage. Neustrelitz 1897. pp. [iv].xv.638+[ii].639–1282. [17,500.]

[ANTONIO VALLARDI], Catalogo delle opere araldiche, genealogiche, biografiche e storiche, manoscritti e stampate, componenti l'Archivio araldico Vallardi. Milano 1884. pp.27. [1000.]

GEORGE GATFIELD, Guide to printed books and manuscripts relating to english and foreign heraldry and genealogy. 1892. pp.[iv].646. [17,500.]
300 copies printed; a copy in the Bibliothèque nationale contains ms. notes.

Family History

A FINDING list of genealogies and local history in the Syracuse public library. Syracuse, N.Y. [1903]. pp.131. [3000.]
— [another edition]. List of books on genealogy and heraldry [&c.]. 1910. pp.119. [2500.]

VERZEICHNISS der bücher- und schriftensammlung des Vereins Herold. Berlin 1904. pp.[iv].333. [5000.]
— Nachtrag. Görlitz 1909. pp.[ii].63. [1000.]

CARLO AUGUSTO BERTINI, Codici vaticani riguardanti la storia nobiliare. Roma 1906. pp.118. [1000.]
205 copies printed.

G[ASTON] DU BOSQ DE BEAUMONT, Inventaire sommaire des archives des généalogistes de l'Ordre souverain de Saint-Jean de Jérusalem (Malte). Vannes 1909. pp.[iii].113. [750.]

[BASIL ANDERTON], Catalogue of books and tracts on genealogy & heraldry in the Central public libraries. Newcastle-upon-Tyne 1910. pp. x.68. [1500.]

KATHARINE TWINING MOODY, Genealogical material in the St. Louis public library. St. Louis 1915. pp.[i].224–254. [700.]
[—] — Revised edition. Genealogical material

Family History

and local histories. . . . By Georgia Gambrill. 1953. pp.315. [7500.]

LIST of references on heraldry. Library of Congress: Washington 1919. ff.5. [43.]*

RUDOLF DIMPFEL, Biographische nachschlagewerke, adelslexika, wappenbücher. Systematische zusammenstellung für historiker und genealogen. Leipzig 1922. pp.[iii].128. [3750.]

JACQUES [PIERRE] MEURGEY[, BARON DE TUPIGNY], Bibliographie des travaux relatifs aux armoiries des provinces et villes de France et de quelques pays étrangers. 1929 [1930]. pp.142.5. [1011.]
— Supplément. [1930]. pp.7. [22.]

CATALOGUE de la bibliothèque de la Société suisse d'héraldique. Fribourg 1930. pp.[v].105. [1200.]
— Supplément. Lausanne 1945. pp.64. [600.]

EXHIBITION of genealogical and heraldic records held at Chaucer house. Society of genealogists: 1937. pp.40. [273.]

[ADLORE] HAROLD LANCOUR, Heraldry. A guide to reference books. Public library: New York 1938. pp.7. [60.]

Family History

PAUL BUHROW, Das genealogische schrifttum in der stadtbücherei. Erfurt 1939. ff.[ii].130 [sic,135]. [2500.]★

KATALOG over genealogisk samlung. Kommunebibliothek: Frederiksberg 1944. pp.98. [1124.]
— Tillæg. 1951. pp.52. [750.]

GUIDES to genealogical research: a selected list. Library of Congress: Washington 1948. single leaf. [6.]★

OLEN C. JEFFRIES, Heraldry, insignia, decorations, crests, medals. Artillery & guided missile school: Library: Special bibliography (no.2): Fort Sill, Okla. 1955. pp.[ii].22. [125.]★
— — — [another edition]. By Margaret D. Kerns. 1960. pp.[ii].20. [200.]★

BENITO MUNICIO CRISTÓBAL and LUIS GARCÍA CUBERO, Bibliografía heráldico-genealógico-nobiliaria de la biblioteca nacional de Madrid. Impresos. Madrid 1958. pp.347+431. [4586.]

JOSEPH JACQUART, Une bibliothèque de généalogiste-amateur. Un inventaire — un plan. Bibliographie internationale 1898–1958. Bruxelles 1959. ff.[ii].vi.35. [175.]★

Family History

AMADEO DELAUNET [Y ESNAOLA], Catálogo de una biblioteca de genealogía y heráldica. San Sebastián 1960. pp.xix.288. [1801.]

ELLEN C. BARRETT, Heraldica... in the Genealogy division of the Los Angeles public library. Redondo Beach 1963. ff.[44]. [357.]*

3. Countries

Austria

COUNT [FRANÇOIS] JOSEPH DE SAINT-GENOIS [DE GRAND-BREUCO], Inventaire des contrats de mariage, testamens et aditions d'héritage, déposés à la table du droit du pays de la Basse-Autriche à Vienne. Vienne 1788. pp.[viii].94. [500.]

FERDINAND KRACKOWIZER, Das archiv von Schlüsselberg im Oberösterr. landes-archiv zu Linz. Oberösterreichischer landes-ausschuss: Linz 1899. pp.97. [1000.]

RUDOLF VON GRANICHSTAEDTEN-CZERVA, Bibliographische quellen zur tiroler familienforschung (tiroler bauern, bürger, edelleute). Quellenbücher zur sippenforschung (vol.i): Görlitz 1939. pp.xv 272. [5000.]

Family History

Belgium

[see also *Netherlands*]

JACQUES STIENNON, Archéologie, épigraphie, héraldique liégeoises. Le fonds Paul Lohest. Bibliotheca universitatis leodiensis: Publications (no.12): Liège 1962. pp.67. [large number.]

CÉCILE DOUXCHAMPS-LEFÈVRE, Inventaire des archives de Corroy-le-Château. Archives de l'état à Namur: Bruxelles 1962. pp.[ii].465. [4567.]

Brazil

[CARLOS FOUQUET], Guía das publicações do Instituto genealógico brasileiro, 1939–1946. São Paulo 1947. pp.3–198. [5000.]

Cuba

CATALOGO de los mapas, planos, croquis y árboles genealógicos existentes en el Archivo nacional de Cuba. Archivo nacional de Cuba: Publicaciones (vol.xxxi &c.): La Habana 1951 &c.
details of this work are entered under Cuba, above.

Denmark

KR[ISTIAN SOFUS AUGUST] ERSLEV, Privatarkiver fra det 19. aarhundrede beroende i Rigsarkivet.

Family History

Rigsarkiv: Vejledende arkivregistraturer (vol.iv): København 1923. pp.[viii].95. [10,000.]

ERIK KROMAN, Privatarkiver før 1660 i Rigsarkivet. Rigsarkiv: Vejledende arkivregistraturer (vol.viii): København 1948. pp.xv.188. [250,000.]

Flanders

ARTHUR [MARIE AUGUSTE CHARLES] MERGHELYNCK, Cabinet des titres de généalogie et d'histoire de la ouest-Flandre et des régions limitrophes. Tournai 1896–1897. pp.xii.634. [555.]

France

[PIERRE L. J.] BÉTENCOURT, Noms féodaux ou noms de ceux qui ont tenu fiefs en France.... depuis le XIIe siècle jusque vers le milieu du XVIIIe. 1826. pp.[iv].xiv.546+[iii].547–1048. [12,500.]

— — Deuxième édition. 1867. pp.15.xv.240+[iii].261+[iii].237+[iii].241. [12,500.]

JOANNIS GUIGARD, Bibliothèque héraldique de la France. 1861. pp.[iii].xxiv.527. [5014.]

LOUIS DE LA ROQUE and ÉDOUARD BARTHÉLEMY, Catalogue des certificats de noblesse délivrés par [Bernard] Chérin pour le service militaire, 1781–1789. 1864. pp.35. [1000.]

Family History

LÉONCE LEX, Rapport sur le service des Archives . . . exercice 1883–1884, contenant l'indication des titres de famille (A–L[M–T]). Département de la Haute-Saône: Vesoul 1884. pp.16+10. [large number.]

G[EORGE EUSTACHE] THOLIN, Catalogue des travaux personnels, dossiers généalogiques, . . . et bibliothèque de madame la comtesse de Raymond, légués . . . aux archives départementales de Lot-et-Garonne. Agen 1889. pp.xxxiv.316. [5000.]
a copy containing supplementary material is in the Bibliothèque nationale.

VISCOUNT A. DE BIZEMONT, Bibliographie nobiliaire de la Lorraine. Nancy 1897. pp.[iv].86. [363.]

BARON [AUGUSTE] DU ROURE, Inventaire analytique de titres & documents originaux tirés des archives du château de Barbegal. 1903. pp.[iii].xiv.537. [250.]
162 copies printed.

J[OSEPH HIPPOLYTE] ROMAN, Bibliographie de l'œuvre généalogique de Guy Allard. Grenoble [printed] 1905. pp.24.

PH[ILIPPE] LAUER, Catalogue des manuscrits de la collection Clairambault. Bibliothèque nationale: 1923–1932. pp.[iii].431+[iii].437+xxxvi. 422. [20,000.]

G[EORGES] A[BEL RENÉ] SIMON, Les études généalogiques en Normandie depuis le XVIIe siècle, suivi d'un essai de bibliographie normande. Caen 1926. pp.73. [500.]

NOËL BECQUART, Répertoire numérique de la sous-série 2E (titres féodaux — titres de famille). Archives départementales de la Dordogne: Périgueux 1936 &c.
the title is incorrect; this is more than a numerical index; in progress.

[PAUL ADAM], Catalogue des armoriaux français imprimés. [1946]. pp.11. [34.]

JACQUES MEURGEY DE TUPIGNY, Guide des recherches généalogiques aux Archives nationales. Avec une étude sur les recherches biographiques aux Archives de la Seine par François de Vaux de Foletier. Direction des archives: 1953. pp.107. [1500.]

LES LIVRES de raison (1328–1870). Exposition ... à la Maison des Chambres d'agriculture. [1954]. pp.36. [110.]

Family History

GASTON SAFFROY, Bibliographie des almanachs et annuaires administratifs, ecclésiastiques et militaires français de l'ancien régime et des almanachs et annuaires généalogiques et nobiliaires du XVIe siècle à nos jours. 1959. pp.iii–xvi.110. [806.]

Germany

JOHANN GEORG L. HESEKIEL, Repertorium für adelsgeschichte. Erstes stück. Verzeichnis von monographieen über die geschichte nicht souverainer fürstlicher, gräflicher, freiherrlicher und adeliger geschlechter. Berlin 1860. pp.x.ff.11–33. [300.]

printed on one side of the leaf.

HANS VON PRITTWITZ UND GAFFRON, Verzeichniss der gedruckten familiengeschichten Deutschlands und der angrenzenden länder und landestheile. Berlin 1882. pp.161. [2000.]

H[EINRICH] REIMER, Kirchenbücher aus den regierungsbezirken Coblenz und Trier. Mitteilungen der K. preussischen archivverwaltung (no.22): Leipzig 1912. pp.[iii].54. [5000.]

RICHARD ROSE, Familiengeschichtliche bibliographie. Heft 1. Allgemeine familiengeschichtliche zeitschriften. Von familien herausgegebene

Family History

zeitschriften und familientagsberichte. Berlin 1917. pp.viii.64. [225.]
no more published.

FAMILIENGESCHICHTLICHE bibliographie. Zentralstelle für deutsche personen- und familiengeschichte: Mitteilungen: Leipzig 1925–1935.

FAMILIENGESCHICHTLICHE quellen. Leipzig.
    i. Herausgegeben von Oswald Spohr. 1926–1930. pp.[iv].76. [30,000.]
    ii. 1927. pp.[ii].196. [100,000.]
    iii. 1928. pp.[iv].148. [70,000.]
    iv. 1929. pp.[ii].238. [100,000.]
    v. 1929–1931. pp.[ii].276. [125,000.]
    vi. 1931–1932. pp.[ii].308. [140,000.]
    vii. 1932–1934. pp.[ii].298. [125,000.]
    viii. 1934–1937. pp.[ii].518. [200,000.]
    ix. 1937–1939. pp.490. [200,000.]
    x. 1939–1942. pp.[ii].574. [250,000.]
    xi. 1942–1947. pp.372. [150,000.]
no more published.

JOHANN JOSEF KENFENHEUER, Alphabetisches namenregister bürgerlicher deutscher wappenvorkommen. Hoffnungsthal-Köln 1937. pp.3–265. [65,000.]

Family History

BARON EGON VON BERCHEM, Heraldische bibliographie... Teil 1. Zentralstelle für deutsche personen- und familiengeschichte: Leipzig 1937. pp. [ii].432. [13,000.]
the works appears to be complete.

GEORG WOLFF, Bücherkunde der fränkischen geschichte. ... Erste abteilung: schrifttum zur geschichte der geschlechter, familien. Gesellschaft für fränkische geschichte: Veröffentlichungen (11th ser.): Würzburg 1937 &c.
in progress?

FRIEDRICH BAMLER, Bibliographie der sippenkunde in Thüringen. Quellenbücher zur sippenforschung (vol.2): Görlitz 1942. pp.xvi.464. [9000.]

SCHRIFTTUMSBERICHTE zur genealogie und zu ihren nachbargebieten. Deutsche arbeitsgemeinschaft genealogischer verbände: Neustadt a. d. Aisch.

 1951–1959. Herausgegeben von... J[ohannes] H[ermann] Mitgau. pp.iv.316. [3000.]

[FRANZ XAVER PRÖLL *and others*], 600 jahre genealogie in Nürnberg. Stadtbibliothek: Ausstellungs-katalog (no.24): Nürnberg 1961. pp. [11]. [110.]

Family History

WILHELM VOLKERT, Schlossarchiv Sandersdorf. Bayerische archivinventare (heft 18): München 1962. pp.xxii.132. [large number.]

HERBERT SPRUTH, Landes- und familiengeschichtliche bibliographie für Pommern. Genealogie und landesgeschichte (vol.ii): Neustadt a. d. Aisch 1962 &c.
in progress.

Great Britain

a. General

CALENDARIUM rotulorum chartarum et inquisitionum ad quod damnum. [Commissioners on public records:] 1803. pp.[vii].596. [20,000.]

THOMAS MOULE, Bibliotheca heraldica Magnæ Britanniæ. An analytical catalogue of books on genealogy, heraldry, nobility, knighthood, & ceremonies. With a list of provincial visitations... and other manuscripts; and a supplement, enumerating the principal foreign genealogical works. 1822. pp.xxiii.668. [1500.]
the author's working copy, containing voluminous ms. additions, is in the British museum.

[SIR CHARLES GEORGE YOUNG], Catalogue of works on the peerage of England, Scotland, and

Family History

Ireland. In the library of C. G. Young. 1826. pp.36. [125.]

—— [another edition]. 1828. pp.88. [200.]
privately printed.

ROBERT CHAMBERS, Index to heirs at law & next of kin: comprising . . . advertisements which have been published during the last 50 years. 1847. pp.[iii].224. [10,000.]

—— Fourth edition . . . by Edward Preston. [1878]. pp.[iii].414. [50,000.]

——— Supplement. 1888. pp.96. [10,000.]

C[ONSTANTINE] W[ILLIAM] DE BERNARDY, De Bernardy's index register for next of kin, heirs at law, legatees and of unclaimed property in Great Britain, the colonies and on the continent, from 1754 to 1856. 1858. pp.vi.414. [40,000.]
reissued without date.

JOHN CAMDEN HOTTEN, A hand-book to the topography and family history of England and Wales. [1863]. pp.viii.368. [8000.]

GUN's list of next of kin & heirs, &c. wanted for unclaimed money, property, &c., who have been advertised for. 1864–1882.

various parts, issues, editions, special lists, etc. of

Family History

this work appeared under various changes of titles, indexing about 75,000 advertisements in all.

CHARLES ROBERTS, Calendarium genealogicum. Henry III. and Edward I. 1865. pp.[ii].lxi.456+ [ii].455–934. [5000.]

[GEORGE WILLIAM MARSHALL], A catalogue of books in the library of George W. Marshall. 1866. pp.[ii].16. [250.]

INDEX to the first seven volumes of the Dodsworth mss. Oxford 1879. pp.[ii].ff.[159]. [20,000.] *privately printed.*

GEORGE W[ILLIAM] MARSHALL, The genealogist's guide to printed pedigrees. Being a general search through genealogical, topographical, and biographical works relating to the United Kingdom, together with references to family histories, peerage claims, etc. 1879. pp.x.514. [25,000.]
— — [another edition]. Guildford [printed] 1903. pp.xiii.880. [40,000.]
— — — J[ohn] B[each] Whitmore, A genealogical guide. An index to british pedigrees in continuation of Marshall. London 1953. pp.xxxiii. 658. [30,000.]

Family History

F. H. DOUGAL & CO., Next of kin, heirs at law, legatees, &c., &c. Index to advertisements, for claimants to vast sums of money and property in Great Britain and the colonies, since 1700. [1879]. pp.68. [15,000.]

— — Fifth edition. Index register to next of kin ... since 1698. [1880]. pp.[ii].128. [30,000.]

— — Eighth edition. Index to advertisements [&c.]. [1888]. pp.[iv].256. [75,000.]

— — Twelfth edition. [1910]. pp.[ii].480. [125,000.]

A CATALOGUE of the library collected by John Stansfeld, Leeds, comprising a complete series of county histories and local topographies ... heraldic and genealogical publications. 1882. pp.[ii].228.61. [1000.]
privately printed.

WALTER RYE, Records and record searching. A guide to the genealogist and topographer. 1888. pp.[iii].ii.ii.204. [very large number.]

— — Second edition. 1897. pp.viii.253. [very large number.]

W[ILLIAM] P[HILLIMORE] W[ATTS] PHILLIMORE, An index to bills of privy signet, commonly called signet bills, 1584 to 1596 and 1603 to 1624, with a

Family History

calendar of writs of privy seal, 1601 to 1603. British record society: Index library (vol.iv): 1890. pp.xvi.235. [20,000.]

LIST of works relating to British genealogy and local history. New York 1910. pp.366. [genealogy: 2000.]

JOSEPH FOSTER, Grantees of arms named in docquets and patents to the end of the seventeenth century [–1898]. . . . Edited by W. Harry Rylands. Publications of the Harleian society (vols.lxvi–lxviii): 1915–1917. pp.xix.290+vii.iv.209+xl.411. [22,500.]

T[HEODORE] R[ADFORD] THOMSON, A catalogue of british family histories. 1928. pp.viii.158. [1500.]
—— Second edition. 1935. pp.3–202. [2000.]

H. G. HARRISON, A select bibliography of english genealogy, with brief lists for Wales, Scotland and Ireland. 1937. pp.viii.167. [2000.]
printed on one side of the leaf.

J[OHN] B[EACH] WHITMORE, A genealogical guide. Harleian society: Publications (vols.xcix, ci, cii, civ): 1947–1952. pp.xxxviii.176+[iv].177–296+[iv].297–448+[iv].449–653. [25,000.]
also issued in one volume, out of series.

Family History

ANTHONY RICHARD WAGNER, A catalogue of english mediaeval rolls of arms. [Harleian society: Publications (vol.c =)] Aspilogia (vol.i): 1950. pp.xxxiii.178. [150.]

INDEX to the [John] Comber papers. West Sussex record office: Lists and indexes (no.2): Chichester 1955. ff.[i].27. [1000.]*

HERALDRY 1250–1950. An exhibition at the Royal Leamington Spa library, art gallery & museum. [Leamington 1959]. pp.[16]. [77.]

HERALDRY and heraldic documents. A display of items from the Kent archives office, c.1200–1933. [Maidstone 1961]. pp.[ii].23. [74.]*

b. *Inquisitiones post mortem*

CALENDARIUM inquisitionum post mortem sive escaetarum. [Commissioners on public records].
    i. Temporibus regum Hen. III. Ed. 1 & Ed. II. 1806. pp.[vii].534. [15,000.]
    ii. Tempore regis Edwardi III. 1808. pp.[iii]. 580. [15,000.]
    iii. Temporibus regum Ric. II. & Hen. IV. 1821. pp.[iii].511. [15,000.]
    iv. Temporibus regum Hen. V. Hen. VI. Edw. IV. & Ric. III. 1828. pp.[iv].746. [25,000.]

Family History

SIR THOMAS PHILLIPPS, Heredes ex inquisitionibus post mortem, a primo Edwardi I. A.D. 1272 ad decimum septimum Henrici VIti. A.D. 1439. Ex mss. Phillipps, no.6538. Medio-Montanis 1841. pp.[iii].87. [4000.]
25 copies printed.

SIR THOMAS PHILLIPPS, Index inquisitionum post mortem, ab anno 1 Hen. 7. ad annum 20 Car. 1. Medio-Montanis 1865. pp.[ii].14.29.11.20.10.19. 44.48.44. [25,000.]

[C. G. CRUMP and J. A. W. CHAPMAN], List of inquisitions ad quod damnum. Public record office: Lists and indexes (nos.xvii, xxii): 1904–1906. pp.lv.410+xliii.411–876. [10,000.]

CALENDAR of inquisitions post mortem and other analogous documents preserved in the Public record office.
    i. Henry III. [By J. E. E. S. Sharp]. 1904. pp. lvi.431. [934.]
    ii. Edward I. [Years 1–19]. 1906. pp.xlix.705. [848.]
    iii. — [20–28]. 1912. pp.xlii.733. [653.]
    iv. — [29–35]. 1913. pp.xliv.511. [470.]
    v. Edward II. [1–9]. 1908. pp.xxiii.603. [629.]
    vi. — [10–20]. 1910. pp.xxxi.688. [766.]

Family History

vii. Edward III. [1–9]. 1909. pp.xlviii.690. [716.]

viii. — [10–20]. 1913. pp.xliv.771. [715.]

ix. — [21–25]. [By E. G. Atkinson]. 1916. pp.xxix.678. [688.]

x. — [26–34]. 1921. pp.xxxvii.803. [668.]

xi. — [35–38]. [Edited by M. C. B. Dawes]. 1935. pp.xxx.680. [629.]

xii. — [39–43]. [Edited by A. E. Stamp]. 1938. pp.xxix.603. [461.]
includes addenda to volumes iii, viii–x.

xiii. — [ ]. [Edited by J. B. W. Chapman and M. C. B. Dawes]. 1954. pp.xxvi.437. [333.]

xiv. — [ ]. 1952. pp.xxiv.554. [355.]

[ ]. Henry VII. [1–12]. [By A. St. J. S. Maskelyne]. 1898. pp.xii.823. [1258.]

[ ]. — [13–20]. 1915. pp.viii.900. [979.]

[ ]. — [ ]. [Edited by M. C. B. Dawes]. 1955. pp.[vii].844. [1185.]

in progress; the volumes for Henry VII, having been published out of sequence, are not numbered.

INDEX of inquisitions. Public record office: Lists and indexes (nos.xxiii, xxvi, xxxii, xxxiii): 1907–1909. pp.[v].358 + [ii].401 + [ii].406 + [iii].449. [50,000.]

Family History

c. *Marriage licences*

[JOSEPH FOSTER], Marriages, 1650 to 1880. Collectanea genealogica (part iv): 1881. pp.64. [2500.]

Aa–Alexander only; no more published.

JOSEPH LEMUEL CHESTER and SIR GEO[RGE] J[OHN] ARMYTAGE, Allegations for marriage licences issued by the dean and chapter of Westminster, 1558 to 1679; also for those issued by the Vicar-general of the archbishop of Canterbury, 1660 to 1679. Publications of the Harleian society (vol.xxiii): 1886. pp.[vii].359. [5000.]

JOSEPH LEMUEL CHESTER and SIR GEO[RGE] J[OHN] ARMYTAGE, Allegations for marriage licences issued from the Faculty office of the archbishop of Canterbury at London, 1543 to 1869. Publications of the Harleian society (vol.xxiv): 1886. pp.[iv].313. [4500.]

SIR GEORGE J[OHN] ARMYTAGE, Allegations for marriage licences issued by the Vicar-general of the archbishop of Canterbury, 1660 to 1669 [–June 1694]. Publications of the Harleian society (vols. xxxiii–xxxiv, xxx–xxxi): 1890, 1892. pp.viii.315 +[iv].284+[v].349+[iv].343. [20,000.]

Family History

JOSEPH MEADOWS COWPER, Canterbury marriage licences. Canterbury.
- i. 1568–1618. 1892. pp.[iv].xii.520. [15,000.]
- ii. 1619–1660. 1894. pp.[iii].viii.coll.1114. pp.1115–1207. [10,000.]
- iii. 1661–1676. 1896. pp.x.coll.528.pp.529–574. [5000.]
- iv. 1677–1700. 1898. pp.x.coll.646.pp.647–713. [7500.]
- v. 1701–1725. 1905. pp.x.coll.628. [7500.]
- vi. 1726–1750. 1906. pp.viii.coll.558. [6000.]

56–108 copies privately printed.

GEO[RGE] E[DWARD] COKAYNE and EDW[ARD] ALEXANDER FRY, Calendar of marriage licences issued by the Faculty office, 1632–1714. British record society: Index library (vol.xxxiii): 1905. pp.[vi].427. [27,500.]

CHA[RLES] A. BERNAU, Sixteenth-century marriages (1538–1600). 1911. pp.[iii].xvi.335. [22,500.]

J. S. W. GIBSON and R. C. COUZENS, Marriage register of Chelsea, Middlesex, 1704–1760. Banbury 1958. pp.[iv].54. [1200.]*

d. *Parish registers*

[F. A. CRISP], List of parish registers edited by Frederick Arthur Crisp. 1886. pp.2. [8].

Family History

—— [another edition]. List of parish registers and other genealogical works [&c.]. 1901. pp. [xiii].92. [50.]

REPORT on the transcription and publication of parish registers, &c. Congress of archæological societies and Society of antiquaries: 1892. pp.16. [500.]
reissued in 1896.
— Second report. . . . With calendar of registers printed and transcribed since the first report. 1896. pp.[ii].18. [600.]

GEORGE W[ILLIAM] MARSHALL, Parish registers: a list of those printed, or of which ms. copies exist in public collections, together with references to extracts therefrom, printed and manuscript. Parish register society (vol.xxx): 1900. pp.iii–viii.133. [4000.]
—— Appendix. 1904. pp.[ii].23. [500.]

GEORGE F. MATTHEWS, Contemporary index to printed parish (and non-parochial) registers . . . with supplementary list of manuscript transcripts to be found in the public libraries of England and Wales. 1908. pp.109. [1500.]

ARTHUR MEREDYTH BURKE, Key to the ancient parish registers of England & Wales. 1908. pp.164.

[very large number.]
—— Supplement. 1909. pp.xiv.
comprises chiefly corrigenda.

CATALOGUE of the parish registers in the possession of the Society of genealogists. 1924. pp.64. [2250.]
—— Second edition. [By Kathleen Blomfield]. 1937. pp.viii.80. [3500.]
interleaved.

PHILLIMORE's parish registers. [List of manuscripts in the custody of Phillimore & co., ltd.] [1937]. pp.8. [400.]

KATHLEEN BLOMFIELD and H. K. PERCY-SMITH, National index of parish register copies. Society of genealogists: 1939. pp.[iv].vi.90. [3500.]*

A LIST of bishop's and other transcripts of parish registers deposited in the library. Central reference library: Southwark 1955. ff.6. [large number.]*

[HENRY J. BROWN], List of modern transcripts of parish registers relating to parishes in the archdeaconry of the east riding of Yorkshire. [Ickenham 1956]. ff.[6]. [125.]*

G[EORG] E[RIC] HASLAM, *ed.* Parish registers, wills. Manchester public libraries: Reference library: Subject catalogue (section 929: genealogy, part 2): Manchester 1957. pp.[91]. [1216.]

e. *Visitations and pedigrees*

INDEX to the heralds' visitations in the British museum. 1823. pp.52. [400.]
—— Second edition. Catalogue of the heralds' visitations; with references to many other valuable genealogical and topographical manuscripts in the British museum. [By Sir Nicholas Harris Nicolas]. 1825. pp.128. [1250.]

[SIR THOMAS PHILLIPPS], Indexes to county visitations in Middle-Hill library. [Middle-Hill] 1840. pp.56. [15,000.]
—— Second edition. 1842. pp.12. [4000.] *incomplete*.

[JAMES COLEMAN], Coleman's general index to printed pedigrees; which are to be found in all the principal county and local histories, and in many privately printed genealogies. 1866. pp.viii. 155. [6000.]

GEORGE W[ILLIAM] MARSHALL, An index to the pedigrees contained in the printed heralds' visitations, etc. etc. 1866. pp.164. [4500.]

Family History

CHARLES BRIDGER, An index to printed pedigrees, contained in county and local histories, the heralds' visitations, and in the more important genealogical collections. 1867. pp.[ii].iv.384. [15,000.]

[JOSEPH FOSTER], Pedigrees contained in the heralds' visitations and other manuscripts in the British museum. Collectanea genealogica (part ii): 1881. pp.128. [6500.]
Abarough-Fleming only; no more published.

JOHN PAUL RYLANDS, Disclaimers at the heralds' visitations. A list of persons who were disclaimed as gentlemen of coat-armour by the heralds at the visitations of the various counties of England. Guildford [printed] 1888. pp.xi.87. [4250.]
100 copies privately printed.

[MALINA ANVERS GILKEY], American and english genealogies in the Library of Congress. Preliminary catalogue. Washington 1910. pp.805. [3800.]
[—] — Second edition. 1919. pp.[iv].1332. [6965.]

LIST of manuscript genealogies in the library of the Lynn historical society. Lynn, Mass. [1958]. ff.7. [264.]★

Family History

f. *Wills and administrations*

[SIR THOMAS PHILLIPPS], Index to names of wills, in P.O. Cant. [Probate office, Canterbury]. [Middle Hill *c*.1840]. pp.24+24. [17,500.]

[JOSEPH FOSTER], An alphabetical hand-list to printed wills, administrations, etc. Collectanea genealogica (part iii): 1881. pp.32. [350.]
Abbot-Barry only; no more published; printed on one side of the leaf.

[JOHN CHALLONER COVINGTON SMITH], Will-registers of the prerogative court of Canterbury, 1384-1840. New-England historic genealogical society: Boston 1892. pp.7. [325.]

INDEX of wills proved in the Prerogative court of Canterbury . . . and now preserved in the Principal probate registry, Somerset house. British record society: Index library (vols.x &c.).
- [i]-ii. 1383-1558. By J[ohn] Challoner C[ovington] Smith . . . (vols.x, xi): 1893-1895.   pp.xxxv.305 + vii.309-699. [30,000.]
- iii. 1558-1583. By S. A. Smith and Leland L. Duncan.... (vol.xviii): 1898. pp.xxvii.433. [14,000.]
- iv. 1584-1604. By S.A. Smith and Edward

Family History

    Alexander Fry. . . . (vol.xxv): 1901. pp. xxiii.568. [17,500.]
- v. 1605–1619. By E. Stokes . . . (vol.xliii): [1905–]1912. pp.viii.611. [25,000.]
- vi. 1620–1629. By R. H. Ernest Hill . . . (vol.xliv): [1908–] 1912. pp.[vii].395. [15,000.]
- vii. 1653–1656. By Thomas M[athews] Blagg and Josephine Skeate Moir . . . (vol.liv): 1925. pp.xx.786. [30,000.]
- viii. 1657–1660. By T. M. Blagg... (vol.lxi): 1936 pp.xv.891. [35,000.]
- ix. 1671–1675. Edited by John Ainsworth ... (vol.lxvii): 1942. pp.xii.292. [10,000.]
- x. 1676–1685. Edited by C[ecil] Harold Ridge . . . (vol.lxxi): 1948. pp.[x].481. [12,500.]

in progress.

WILLIAM BRIGG, Genealogical abstracts of wills, proved in the Prerogative court of Canterbury. Register 'Wootton' 1658. Leeds 1894–1914. pp. [iii].125 + [iii].157 + [ii].143 + [iii].154 + [iii].169+[iv].151+[iv].133. [5000.]
privately printed.

JOHN and GEORGE F. MATTHEWS, 'Year books of probates' (from 1630). Abstracts of probate acts

Family History

in the Prerogative court of Canterbury. [1902–1926]. pp.349+431+292+582+389+506+352. [60,000.]
extends to 1655.

—— Sentences and complete index nominum (probates and sentences) for the years 1630–1639. 1907 [on cover: 1908]. pp.171. [1000.]

—— Abstracts of probates and sentences in the Prerogative court of Canterbury, 1620–24. [Vol.1]. 1911. [1914]. pp.341. [7000.]
no more published.

J. HENRY LEA, Abstracts of wills in the Prerogative court of Canterbury at Somerset house ... register Soame, 1620. New-England historic genealogical society: Boston 1904. pp.xiii.607. [1366.]

REGINALD M. GLENCROSS, Administrations in the Prerogative court of Canterbury, 1559–1571. Exeter [printed] 1912. pp.[iii].167. [1750.]

C. EVELEIGH WOODRUFF, Sede vacante wills: a calendar of wills proved before the commissary of the prior and chapter of Christ church, Canterbury, during vacancies in the primacy. Kent archæological society: Kent records (vol.iii): Canterbury 1914. pp.[ix].xxii.147.vii. [950.]

Family History

HENRY R. PLOMER, Index of wills and administrations now preserved in Probate registry at Canterbury, 1396–1558 and 1640–1650. British record society: Index library (vol.l): 1920. pp.viii.603. [30,000.]

J. H. MORRISON, Prerogative court of Canterbury. Register 'Scroope' (1630). Abstracts and index. 1934. pp.xiii.280. [1363.]*

J. H. MORRISON, Prerogative court of Canterbury. Wills, sentences and probate acts, 1661–1670. 1935. pp.viii.334. [19,492.]*

J. H. MORRISON, Prerogative court of Canterbury. Letters of administration, 1620–1630. . . . Abstracts. 1935. pp.xi.162. [8179.]*

[J. CHALLENOR SMITH], Index of wills recorded in the archiepiscopal registers at Lambeth palace. 1919. pp.88. [1500.]
the British museum contains ms. corrections

ALFRED GUEST, Index to early Exeter wills 1286–1400, from [John] Hooker's commonplace book and preserved in the court rolls of the mayors of Exeter. Compiled . . . from abstracts by miss O. M. Moger. 1956. ff.12. [400.]*

Family History

A LIST of wills and marriage settlements in the local history collection of the Shrewsbury public library. Shrewsbury 1958. pp.[25]. [1000.]*

Hungary

KÁROLY TAGÁNYI, Jegyzéke az országos levéltárban a Magyar és Erdélyi udv. kanczelláriák fölállításáig található Herczegi, Grófi, Bárói, Honossági és Nemesi okleveleknek. Budapest 1886. pp.79. [7500.]

A MAGYAR nemzeti múzeum könyvtárának czímereslevelei. A Magyar nemzeti múzeum könyvtárának czímjegyzéke (vol.ii): Budapest.
  i. 1200–1868. 1904. Leirta Aldásy Antal. pp. xix.494.
  ii. 1092–1600. 1930. pp.160+161–307.
  iii. 1601–1657. Leirta Czobor Alpéd. 1937. pp.xv.503. [1070.]
  iv. 1657–1716. 1938. pp.xi.512. [992.]
  v. 1717–1770. 1939. pp.xi.508. [836.]
  vi. 1771–1800. 1940. pp.xi.608. [594.]
  vii. 1801–1825. 1941. pp.xi.580. [440.]
  viii. 1826–1909. 1942. pp.xv.588. [456.]

Ireland

SIR ARTHUR [EDWARD] VICARS, Index to the

prerogative wills of Ireland, 1536–1810. Dublin 1897. pp.xi.512. [37,500.]

HENRY FARRAR, Irish marriages, being an index to the marriages in Walker's Hibernian magazine, 1771 to 1812. With an appendix from the notes of sir Arthur Vicars . . . of the births, marriages, and deaths in the Anthologia hibernica, 1793 and 1794. 1897. pp.[vii].243+[iii].245–532. [6000.]
75 copies privately printed.

INDEXES to irish wills.
    i. Ossory, Leighlin, Ferns, Kildare. By W[illiam] P[hillimore] W[atts] Phillimore. 1909. pp.viii.142. [5500.]
    ii. Cork and Ross, Cloyne. 1910. pp.vii.154. [6000.]
    iii. Cashel and Emly, Waterford and Lismore, Killaloe and Kilfenora, Limerick, Ardfert and Aghadoe. By Gertrude Thrift. 1913. pp.[vii].153. [6000.]
    iv. Dromore, Newry, and Mourne. 1918. pp.8.178. [7000.]
    v. Derry and Raphoe. 1920. pp.vii.200. [8000.]

INDEX to births, marriages & deaths in a file of the Hibernian chronicle, October 1769–April

1802. Society of genealogists: 1936. ff.[iii].94+[iv].105. [7500.]*

Italy

GIUSTINO COLANERI, Bibliografia araldica e genealogica d'Italia. Roma 1904. pp.xix.155. [2056.]

500 copies printed.

LUIGI RIZZOLI, Manoscritti della Biblioteca civica di Padova riguardanti la storia nobiliare italiana. Roma 1906. pp.125. [20,000.]

ANTON FERRANTE BOSCHETTI, I cataloghi dell'opera di Pompeo Litta 'Famiglie celebri italiane'. Modena 1930. pp.59. [184.]

the volumes are not all by Litta.

ROBERTO RIDOLFI, Gli archivi delle famiglie fiorentine. Firenze 1934. pp.v.246. [1500.]

50 copies printed; no more published.

ANTONIO GHENO, Contributo alla bibliografia genealogica italiana. Collezione di monografie storiche ed artistiche (supplemento alla 'Rivista araldica' 20 Marzo 1936): Roma 1936. pp.iii–viii.297. [5000.]

RAFFAELE AURINI, Dizionario bibliografico della

Family History

gente d'Abruzzo. Teramo [printed] 1952–1958. pp.iii–xvi.479+479+3–479. [12,500.]

Jews

HERMANN M. Z. MEYER, Bibliographia genealogica judaica. Jerusalem 1942. ff.21.
22 copies reproduced from typewriting.

Mauritius

OCTAVE BÉCHET, Inventaire des registres paroissiaux de l'Île de France (île Maurice). Compagnie des Indes, 1722–1767. Port-Louis 1952–1958. pp. 420. [5000.]

Netherlands

J[ULES] HUYTTENS, L'art de vérifier les généalogies des familles belges et hollandaises. Bruxelles 1865. pp.[iii].184. [8000.]

PHILIPPE JEAN BAPTISTE O'KELLY [DE GALWAY], Recueil analytique des édits, placards & ordonnances héraldiques des Pays-Bas espagnols et autrichiens. Publié, d'après un manuscrit, ... par le comte A[lphonse Charles Albert] O'Kelly de Galway ... et Léopold van Hollebeke. Bruges 1865. pp.xiv.122. [200.]
compiled in 1775.

Family History

CATALOGUS der tentoonstelling van voorwerpen betrekking hebbende op het vorstelijk stamhuis Oranje-Nassau en op de wapen-, geslacht- en zegelkunde in het algemeen. 's Gravenhage 1880. pp.viii.472. [5224.]

[JOHAN HENDRICK SCHEFFER], Grafelijke commissie of beveelboeken van hertog Aelbrecht van Beyeren. I. 1392–1404 [II. 1408–1418]. Nederlands familie-archief: Rotterdam 1883. pp.[iv].viii.102 +[v].57. [750.]

CATALOGUS van geslachtkundige werken, wapens, enz. verkrijgbaar ... bij het genealogisch en heraldisch archief te 's-Gravenhage. 's-Gravenhage 1892. pp.75. [500.]

P. N. VAN DOORNINCK, Inventaris van eene verzameling charters betrekking hebbende op de geslachten van der Does, Duvenvoorde, Mathenesse, enz. Haarlem 1895. pp.[iii].92. [169.]
the collection forms part of the archives of the diocese of Haarlem.

HENRI [AUGUSTE] OMONT, Recueils généalogiques du baron de Launay conservés à la Bibliothèque nationale (mss. français 31812–31861). 1897. pp.12. [1000.]

[ELTJO ALDEGONDUS VAN BERESTEYN], Reperto-

rium van gedrukte genealogieën en genealogische fragmenten aangeboden aan het Koninklijk nederlandsch genootschap voor geslacht- en wapenkunde ... door ... E. A. van Beresteyn. Haarlem 1933. pp.224. [188.]
reissued in 1948 under the title of Genealogisch repertorium.

INVENTARIS van de collectie [Alexander Bernhard and Willem Anne] van Spaen. 's-Gravenhage 1951. pp.56. [271.]

F. M. HENDRIKS, Beschrijving van de doop-, trouw- en begraafboeken, de registers van aangegeven lijken enz. in Overijsel, dagtekenende van vóór de invoering van de burgerlijke stand. Rijksarchief in Overijsel [Zwolle]: s'-Gravenhage 1952. pp.133. [large number.]

J. M. VAN DE VENNE, Beschrijving van de doop-, trouw- en degraafboeken (overlijdensregisters) in de provincie Limburg, dagtekenende van vóór de invoering van de burgerlijke stand. Rijksarchief in Limburg: 's Gravenhage 1953. pp.150. [large number.]

A. PATHUIS and E. J. WERKMAN, Beschrijving van de doop-, trouw- en begraafboeken, enz. in de provincies Groningen en Drente, dagtekenende van vóór de invoering van de burgerlijke stand.

Family History

Rijksarchieven in Groningen en Drente: 's-Gravenhage 1953. pp.[ii].125. [large number.]

Norway

GENEALOGEN kjøbmand F[redrik] Bing Bucks testamentariske gave af personal hist. og hist. litteratur. Kgl. norske videnskabers selskab: Trondhjem 1902. pp.[ii].7. [150.]

GUSTAV E[LISAR] RAABE, Norske stamtavler. Bibliografi. [Oslo 1941]. pp.127. [1000.]

SLEKTHISTORISK litteratur. Kommunebibliotek: Stavanger 1943.
— — Tilvekst 1943–55. 1955. pp.64. [1750.]

GUSTAV E[LISAR] RAABE, Norsk slektshistorisk litteratur utkommet i 1945. [Oslo 1946]. pp.29. [100.]
125 copies printed.

Poland

ADAM WOLFF, Mazowieckie zapiski herbowe z XV i XVI wieku. Akademia umiejętności: Rody ziemiańskie XV i XVI wieku: Kraków 1937. pp. xx.382. [1084.]

Portugal

INVENTARIO dos livros de matricula dos mora-

Family History

dores da Casa real. Volume I. 1641 a 1681. Archivo nacional Torre do tombo: Lisboa 1911. pp.[iii]. 432. [4000.]

EDUARDO DE CAMPOS DE CASTRO DE AZEVEDO SOARES, Bibliographia nobiliarchica portugueza. Braga 1916–1923. pp.213+242+176. [3126.]
250 copies privately printed.

Prussia

MAX BÄR, Der adel und der adlige grundbesitz in Polnisch-Preussen zur zeit der preussischen besitzergreifung. Nach auszügen aus den vasallenlisten und grundbüchern. Mitteilungen der K. preussischen archivverwaltung (no.19): Leipzig 1911. pp.xi.274. [2500.]

Russia

ALEKSANDR [PLATONOVICH] BARSUKOV, Обзоръ источниковъ и литературы русскаго родословія. Записки Имп. академіи наукъ (vol.liv, no.4): Санкт-Петербугръ 1887. pp.[ii]. 96. [200.]

L[EONID] M[IKHAILOVICH] SAVELOV, Опытъ библіографическаго указателя по исторіи

Family History

и генеалогіи россійскаго дворянства. Москва 1893. pp.[iii].56[*sic*, 156]. [756.]
40 copies printed.

—— Изданіе второе. Библіографическій указатель по исторіи, геральдикѣ и родословію россійскаго дворянства. Острогожк 1897. pp.269. [1098.]

L[EONID] M[IKHAILOVICH] SAVELOV, Избранная библіотека русскаго генеалога. (Библіографическій опытъ). Выпускъ первый. Москва 1895. pp.25. [48.]
100 copies printed; no more published?

L[EONID] M[IKHAILOVICH] SAVELOV, Библіографическій указатель по исторіи, геральдикѣ и родословію тульскаго дворянства. Москва 1904. pp.[ii].xv.412. [1280.]

L[EONID] M[IKHAILOVICH] SAVELOV, Генеалогическія рѣдкости'. Списокъ рѣдкихъ и замѣчательныхъ изданій по русской генеалогіи. Москва 1904. pp.[ii].ii.32. [111.]

Scotland

[WILLIAM BARCLAY TURNBULL], Catalogue of manuscripts relating to genealogy and heraldry,

Family History

preserved in the library of the Faculty of advocates, at Edinburgh. 1852. pp.24. [400.]
10 copies privately printed.

FRANCIS J. GRANT, The commissariat record of Hamilton and Campsie. Register of testaments, 1564–1800. British record society (Scottish section): Index library (vol.xx): Edinburgh 1898. pp.iv.85. [3750.]

JOHN ANDERSON, Calendar of the Laing charters, A.D. 854–1837, belonging to the university of Edinburgh. Edinburgh 1890. pp.vii.1053. [3326.]

INDEX to general register of sasines, 1701–1720. Record office, Scotland: Indexes (no.2): Edinburgh 1917. pp.[ii].iv.882 [25,000.]

INDEX to register of deeds. Record office, Scotland: Indexes (no.1 &c.): Glasgow [Edinburgh].
    i. 1661 . . . (no.17): 1929. pp.[iv].532. [16,000.]
    ii. 1662 . . . (no.19): 1931. pp.[iv].631. [18,000.]
    iii. 1663 . . . (no.1): 1915. pp.[iv].505. [15,000.]
    iv. 1664 . . . (no.2): 1917. pp.[iv].489. [14,000.]

Family History

v. 1665 . . . (no.4): 1921. pp.[iv].484. [14,000.]

vi. 1666 . . . (no.5): 1921. pp.[iv].508. [15,000.]

vii. 1667 . . . (no.6): 1923. pp.[iv].456. [13,000.]

viii. 1668 . . . (no.8): 1924. pp.[iv].475. [14,000.]

ix. 1669 . . . (no.10): 1926. pp.[iv].491. [14,000.]

x. 1670 . . . (no.11): 1926. pp.[iv].465. [13,000.]

xi. 1671 . . . (no.14): 1928. pp.[iv].465. [13,000.]

xii. 1672 . . . (no.20): 1931. pp.[iv].417. [12,000.]

xiii. 1673 . . . (no.22): 1931. pp.[iii].363. [10,000.]

xiv. 1674 . . . (no.24): 1933. pp.[iv].362. [10,000.]

xv. 1675 . . . (no.26): 1934. pp.[iv].407. [12,000.]

xvi. 1676 . . . (no.28): 1934. pp.[iv].403. [12,000.]

xvii. 1677 . . . (no.30): 1935. pp.[iv].373. [11,000.]

Family History

xviii. 1678 . . . (no.32): 1938. pp.[iv].382. [11,000.]
xix. 1679 . . . (no.34): 1939. pp.[iv].454. [11,000.]*
xx. 1680 . . . (no.35): 1952. pp.[iii].533. [13,000.]*

in progress.

MARGARET STUART, Scottish family history. A guide to works of reference on the history and genealogy of scottish families. Edinburgh 1930. pp.vii.386. [6000.]

SCOTTISH family histories. A list of books for consultation in the reference library. Public libraries: Edinburgh 1951. pp.40. [750.]
— Supplement. 1953. ff.[i].8. [125.]*

JOAN P. S. FERGUSON, Scottish family histories held in scottish libraries. Scottish central library: Edinburgh 1960. pp.xiii.195. [2000.]

Spain

G[ERHARD] E[RNEST] [FRANCK] VON FRANCKENAU, Bibliotheca hispanica historico-genealogico-heraldica. Lipsiæ 1724. pp.[viii].412.[xxvii]. [1490.]
a contemporary ms. note in the Bodleian library

Family History

copy states that 'El verdadero Autor de este Libro fue Don Juan Lucas Cortes, A. de Sancha'.

CIRIACO MIGUEL VIGIL, Heráldica asturiana y catálogo armorial de España, seguidos de . . . la bibliografía del blasón, órdenes de caballería y genealogías. Apuntes heraldicos: Oviedo 1892. pp.397. [6000.]

VICENTE CASTAÑEDA Y ALCOVER, Índice sumario de los manuscritos castellanos de genealogía, heráldica y órdenes militares que se custodian en la Real biblioteca de San Lorenzo del Escorial. Madrid 1917. pp.96. [101.]

[JUAN XIMÉNEZ DE EMBÚN and ANGEL GONZÁLEZ PALENCIA], Catálogo alfabético de los documentos referentes a títulos del reino y grandezas de España conservados en la sección de Consejos suprimidos. Archivo histórico nacional: Madrid 1919. pp.vii.739. [6000.]

CATÁLOGO alfabético de los documentos referentes a hidalguías conservados en la sección de consejos suprimidos. Archivo histórico nacional: Madrid 1920. pp.158. [3000.]

ALFREDO BASANTA DE LA RIVA, Catálogo de todos sus pleitos, expedientes y probanzas, formado directamente de los documentos. Archivo de la Real chancillería de Valladolid: Sala de los hijosdalgo: Valladolid 1920–1922. pp.435+451+438+320. [60,000.]

MARIANO ALCOCER Y MARTÍNEZ, Catálogo de privilegios y mercedes de hidalguía. Archivo general de Simancas (catálogo xi): Valladolid 1927. pp.434. [3797.]

ANGEL GONZÁLEZ PALENCIA, Mayorazgos españoles. Biblioteca histórica y genealógica (vol.i): Madrid 1929. pp.iii–xiii.351. [970.]
limited to the documents in the Registro general del sello de Castilla, preserved in the Archivo histórico nacional in Madrid; 300 copies printed.

JOSÉ ANTONIO MARTÍNEZ BARA, Catálogo de fondos genealógicos. Archivo histórico de Huesca: Madrid 1952. pp.141. [1500.]

A[NTONIO R.] RODRÍGUEZ-MOÑINO, Catálogo de los manuscritos genealogicos de Blas de Salazar. Valencia 1952. pp.85. [141.]
100 copies printed.

MIGUEL SANTIAGO RODRÍGUEZ, Documentos y manuscritos genealógicos. Dirección general de archivos y bibliotecas: Guías de archivos y bibliotecas: Madrid 1954. pp.689. [6000.]

Family History

FLORENCIO AMADOR CARRANDI, Catálogo de genealogías. Excma dipvtación de Vizcaya: Casa de juntas de Guernica: Archivo: [Bilbao] 1958. pp.[vi].1043. [2576.]

ENRIQUE DE OCERÍN [Y GARCÍA], Índice de los expedientes matrimoniales de militares y marinos que se conservan en el Archivo general militar (1761–1865). Consejo superior de investigaciones científicas: Instituto Jerónimo Zurita: Genealogía y heráldica (vol.vii): Madrid 1959– . pp. iii–lxxiii.687+

in progress.

AMADEO DELAUNET [ESNAOLA], Catálogo de una biblioteca de genealogía y heráldica. San Sebastián 1960. pp.v–xix.288. [1801.]

Sweden

JOH[AN] AX[EL] ALMQUIST, Svensk genealogisk litteratur. Svenska autograf sällskap: Skrifter och handlingar (vol.vii): Stockholm 1905. pp.78. [455.]

Switzerland

JEAN GRELLET and MAURICE TRIPET, Heraldik und genealogie. Centralkommission für schweizerische landeskunde: Bibliographie der schwei-

Family History

zerischen landeskunde (section v.4): Bern 1895. pp.x.56. [1100.]

United States

WILLIAM H[ENRY] WHITMORE, A handbook of american genealogy: being a catalogue of family histories and publications containing genealogical information. Albany, [N.Y.] 1862. pp.272. [250.]
100 copies printed.

—— Fifth edition. The american genealogist [&c.]. 1900. pp.406. [2750.]
a copy in the library of Congress contains numerous additions in manuscript.

DANIEL S[TEELE] DURRIE, Bibliographia genealogica americana: an alphabetical index to american genealogies and pedigrees contained in state, county and town histories, printed genealogies, and kindred works. Albany, N.Y. 1868. pp.xii.5–296. [10,000.]

—— Fifth edition. Index to american genealogies. 1900. pp.352. [45,000.]

——— Supplement, 1900–1908. 1908. pp.107. [12,500.]
a new edition was begun in 1933 but was not completed.

MORTIMER DELANO DE LANNOY, The bibliography of american heraldry. New York 1896. pp.12. [31.]

THOMAS ALLEN GLENN, A list of some american genealogies which have been printed in book form. Philadelphia 1897. pp.[v].71. [2000.]

LIST of titles of genealogical articles in american periodicals and kindred works. Albany, N.Y. 1899. pp.165. [1500.]

A LIST of genealogies in preparation. New England historic genealogical society: Boston 1906. pp.27. [600.]

FINDING list of works on genealogy and american local history in Michigan state library. Michigan state library: Bulletin (no.7): Lansing 1906. pp.[ii].128. [2000.]
— Second edition. Genealogy [&c.]. 1915. pp. [ii].169. [3250.]

THE GRAFTON index of titles of books and magazine articles on history, genealogy and biography printed in the United States on american subjects during the year 1909. New York [1910]. pp.68. [2000.]

[MALINA ANVERS GILKEY], American and english genealogies in the Library of Congress. Prelimi-

Family History

nary catalogue. Washington 1910. pp.805. [3800.]
[—] — Second edition. 1919. pp.[iv].1332. [6965.]

LIST of family genealogies in library of Connecticut historical society. Hartford 1911. pp.30. [1600.]
— [another edition]. 1911. pp.42. [1900.]

GEORGIA L. OSBORNE, A list of the genealogical works in the Illinois state historical library, Springfield. Illinois state historical library: Publication (no.xviii): [Springfield] 1914. pp.163. [1000.]
— — Supplement ... (no.xxiii): 1919. pp.182. [1500.]

LIST of references on american genealogy and family names. Library of Congress: Washington 1915. ff.3. [25.]*

CHECK LIST of collections of personal papers in historical societies, university and public libraries, and other learned institutions in the United States. Library of Congress: Washington 1918. pp.87. [large number.]

DONALD LINES JACOBUS, Index to genealogical periodicals. Baltimore 1932 &c.
in progress.

Family History

EMMA TOEDTEBERG, Catalogue of american genealogies in the library of the Long Island historical society. Brooklyn 1935. pp.[viii].660. [9051.]

ROSALIE FELLOWS BAILEY, Guide to genealogical and biographical sources for New York city (Manhattan) 1783–1898. New York [1954]. pp. iv.96. [1000.]

an earlier edition appeared in the New England historical and genealogical register *(1952–1954), cvi–cviii.*

WALLACE R. DRAUGHON, North Carolina genealogical reference. A research guide. Durham 1956. pp.[vii].231]. [large number.]

INEZ WALDENMAIER, A finding list of Virginia marriage records before 1853. [Washington 1956]. pp.[vi].12. [large number.]*
—— [another edition]. [1957]. pp.[iii].44. [large number.]*

RUTH LONG DOUTHIT, Some references for genealogical searching in Ohio. Detroit society for genealogical research: Detroit 1960. pp.51. [900.]*

FRANKLIN S[HEELY] WEISER, Parochial registers for lutheran congregations in Lancaster county,

Family History

Pennsylvania, 1729–1960. A guide to genealogical resources. Lancaster, Pa. 1961. ff.[i].12. [large number.]

CAROLYNE L. WENDEL, Aids for genealogical searching in Indiana. A bibliography. Detroit society for genealogical research: [Detroit] 1962. pp.[iii].154. [1500.]*

Names.
1. General, 55.
2. Personal names, 57.
3. Place-names, 58.

1. *General*

ONOMA. Bibliographical and information bulletin. International committee of onomastic sciences: Louvain.

    i. 1950. pp.54.89.[i]. [2000.]
    ii. 1951. pp.118.69.[i]. [1500.]
    iii. 1952. pp.196.80.[i]. [2500.]
    iv. 1953. pp.[viii].240.93. [3000.]
    v. 1954. pp.vii.278.79. [3500.]

    vi. 1955–1956. pp.ix.306.68. [4000.]
    vii. 1956–1957. pp.
    viii. 1958–1959. pp.[vii].518.82. [6000.]
    ix. 1960–1961. pp.[iii].366.110.47. [5000.]
    x. 1962–1963. pp.[iii].251. [9000.]
in progress.

Names

JOHANNES HUBSCHMID, Bibliographia onomastica helvetica. Bibliothèque nationale: Bibliographica helvetica: Berne 1954. pp.viii.50. [800.]
also issued as a supplement to Onoma (*Louvain 1952*), *iii*.

G[EORG] E[RIC] HASLAM, ed. Personal and place names, epitaphs, heraldry, flags. Manchester public libraries: Reference library: Subject catalogue (section 929: genealogy, part 3): Manchester 1958. pp.[79]. [1407.]

WITOLD TASZYCKI, MIECZYSŁAW KARAS and ADAM TURASIEWICZ, Bibliografia onomastyki polskiej do roku 1958 włącznie. Uniwersytet jagielloński: Wydawnictwa (vol.62): Kraków 1960. pp.[iii].xxii.337. [3200.]

R[ICHARD] J[ULIAN] ROBERTS, Bibliography of writings on english place- and personal names. International committee of onomastic sciences: Onoma (vol.viii, part 3): Louvain 1961. pp.[v].82. [1233.]

WITOLD TASZYCKI, Bibliographie de l'onomastique polonaise jusqu'en 1960 (inclusivement). Onoma (vol.ix, no.3): Louvain 1963. pp.[iii].110. [1472.]

Names

2. Personal names

WILLIAM GEORGE SEARLE, Onomasticon anglo-saxonicum. A list of anglo-saxon proper names from the time of Beda to that of king John. Cambridge 1897. pp.lix.602. [17,500.]

W[ILLIAM] P[HILLIMORE] W[ATTS] PHILLIMORE and E[DWARD] A[LEXANDER] FRY, An index to changes of name . . . 1760 to 1901. 1905. pp.xxxii.357. [5000.]

F. K. and S. HITCHING, References to english surnames in 1601 [1602]. Walton-on-Thames [vol.ii: London] 1910–1911. pp.lxx + xcv. [22,500.]

LIST of references on personal names. Library of Congress: Washington 1920. ff.6. [62.]*
— Additional references. 1922. ff.2. [16.]*

K. ROELANDTS, De persoonsnamenstudie in 1947. Vereeniging voor naamkunde te Leuven: Mededelingen: Bijlagen (no.xxvi): Leuven 1948. pp.[i].247–272. [100.]

ELSDON C[OLES] SMITH, Personal names. A bibliography. Public library: New York 1952. pp.226. [3415.]

Names

3. Place-names

GEORG BUCHNER, Die ortsnamenkundliche literatur von Südbayern. Mit einem anhang: ortsnamenkundliche literatur aus den übrigen kreisen. München 1920. pp.28. [350.]

GEORG BUCHNER, Bibliographie zur ortsnamenkunde der Ostalpenländer. München 1927. pp.36. [1500.]

H[ENDRIK] J[OZEF] VAN DE WIJER, Bibliographie van de vlaamsche plaatsnaamkunde. Vlaamsche toponymische vereeniging: Nomina geographica flandrica (no.1): 's-Gravenhage 1928. pp.xxvi.157. [1250.]

EMIL MEYNEN, Amtliche und private ortsnamenverzeichnisse des Grossdeutschen reiches und der mittel- und osteuropäischen nachbargebiete 1910–1941. Berichte zur deutschen landeskunde (special no.1): Leipzig 1942. pp.162. [600.]

SELECTED bibliography of gazetteers and place name materials: theatre areas M [Europe] and N [U.S.S.R.]. Army map service: Washington 1943. ff.[i].v.ii.107. [400.]*

RICHARD B[URL] SEALOCK and PAULINE A[UGUSTA] SEELY, Bibliography of place name literature: United States, Canada, Alaska and Newfoundland.

Names

American library association: Chicago 1948. pp.[x].332. [2500.]*

CATALOG of publications. Board on geographic names: Washington 1949. pp.[vi].11. [200.]
— [another edition]. 1953. pp.[vi].20. [250.]

ELLIS DAVIES, Flintshire place-names. Cardiff 1959. pp.xi.184. [2000.]

JOAQUIM DA SILVEIRA, Indice geral dos artigos de toponímia portuguesa. Universidade de Coimbra: Faculdade de letras: Instituto de estudos românicos: Coimbra 1959. pp.52. [1250.]

SELECTED bibliography on canadian toponymy. Department of mines and technical surveys: Geographical branch: Bibliographical series (no.30): Ottawa 1964. pp.[iv].27. [500.]*

Family Names

Almquist, family of.

JOH. AX. ALMQUIST, Almquistiana, eller förteckning på de tryckta arbeten, som författats eller utgifvits af medlemmar af den från Kyrkovärden Erich Abrahamsson i Löfsta af Almunge socken och Upland härstammande slägten Almquist. Upsala [printed] 1892. pp.xii.295. [665.]
100 copies printed.

Arbuthnot, family of.

[GEORGE HOME], Inventory of Arbuthnot titles, from 1206 to 1483. [Edited by James Maidment]. [Edinburgh 1822]. pp.24. [62.]
16 copies privately printed; some of these were bound up in [James Maidment and Robert Pitcairn], Nugae derelictae, Edinburgi 1822.

Argenti, family of.

[PHILIP PANTELES ARGENTI], Family letters. [s.l. c.1930]. pp.6+8+8. [258.]

Family Names

[—] Calendar of documents from records in the Coraïs library, Chios (coies), relating to members of the Argenti family, 1840–1911 and 1929. [*c.*1930]. pp.13. [87.]

[—] Calendar of documents from italian archives (official copies) relating to the Argenti family. [*c.*1930]. pp.18. [72.]

[—] Calendar of Argenti family documents. I. 1402–1920 (II. 1306, 1556, 1725–1931). [*c.*1930]. pp.4+4. [171.]

Ashburnham, family of.

FRANCIS W[ILLIAM] STEER, The Ashburnham archives. A catalogue. East Sussex county council: Lewes 1958. pp.xxiv. 144. [10,000.]

Bach, family of.

VERZEICHNISS des musikalischen nachlasses des verstorbenen capellmeisters Carl Philipp Emanuel Bach. Hamburg 1790. pp.[ii].142. [1000.]

reprinted in the Bach-jahrbuch (*1938–1948*), *xxxv–xxxvii.*

SYLVIA W. KENNEY [*and others*], Catalog of the Emilie and Karl Riemenschneider memorial Bach library. Baldwin-Wallace college: New York 1960. pp.xvii.295. [2537.]

Family Names

Backer, family of.

I[SABELLE] H[ENRIETTE] VAN EEGHEN, Inventaris van het familie-archief Backer. Archief der gemeente: [Amsterdam]. 1954. pp.114. [10,000.]

Bagshawe, family of.

F[RANK] TAYLOR, Hand-list of the Bagshawe muniments deposited in the John Rylands library. Manchester 1955. pp.[ii].144. [10,000.]

Baker, family of.

[CHARLES EDWARD BAKER], A catalogue of autographs, books, manuscripts, . . . connected with the several families of the name of Baker, now in the possession of Charles Edward Baker. Nottingham 1907. pp.33. [700.]

Bastard, family of.

[VISCOUNT HENRI DE BASTARD D'ESTANG], Inventaire de sources historiques, manuscrites et imprimées . . . pour servir de preuves à la généalogie de la maison de Bastard. 1847. pp.162. [3500.]

Bathurst, family of.

[FRANCIS BICKLEY], Report on the manuscripts

Family Names

of earl Bathurst. Royal commission on historical manuscripts: 1923. pp.xx.788. [1500.]

Baux, family of.

L[OUIS] BARTHÉLEMY, Inventaire chronologique et analytique des chartes de la maison de Baux. Marseille 1882. pp.xxxi.680. [2000.]

Bentinck, family of.

S[ANDFORD] ARTHUR STRONG, A catalogue of letters and other historical documents exhibited in the library at Welbeck. 1903. pp.xvi.316. [100.]

Berkeley, family of.

ISAAC HERBERT JEAYES, Descriptive catalogue of the charters and muniments in the possession of... lord Fitzhardinge, at Berkeley castle. Bristol 1892. pp.[vii].xxxix.443. [1500.]

Bernadotte, house of.

[HARALD OSSIAN WIESELGREN], En kunglig familjs bibliografi. [Stockholm 1867]. pp.46. [300.]

Bessay, family of.

COUNT FRANÇOIS DE BESSAY, Inventaire des titres

Family Names

de la maison de Bessay. [Poitiers] 1665. pp.28.
[125.]

Bicker, family of.

I[SABELLE] H[ENRIETTE] VAN EEGHEN, Inventaris
van het familie-archief Bicker. Gemeentelijke archiefdienst: [Amsterdam] 1956. pp.142. [20,000.]

Bilderdijk, family of.

[G.], Lijst der werken uitgegeven door of met
bijdragen voorzien van wijlen m^r W. Bilderdijk,
en v^e K. W. Bilderdijk. Amsterdam 1833. pp.xii.
163. [4000.]

B[ASTIAN] KLINKERT, Lijst der werken, geschreven door of met bijdragen voorzien van wijlen
m^r. Willem Bilderdijk, en vrouwe Katharina
Wilhelmina Bilderdijk. [De navorscher (1853,
bijvoegsel): Amsterdam 1853]. pp.[ii].iv.30. [1000.]

CATALOGUS der verzamelingen Bilderdijk en van
Lennep, aanwezig in de boekerij der Koninklijke
akademie van wetenschappen. Amsterdam 1887.
pp.iv.137. [Bilderdijk: 468.]

Bodman, family of.

A. POINSIGNON, Bodman'sche regesten. [Verein

Family Names

für geschichte des Bodensee's und seiner umgebung: Schriften (nos.10–12: anhang)]: Lindau 1880–1883. pp.66. [295.]

[BARON LEOPOLD VON BODMAN], Geschichte der freiherrn von Bodman. [1. Urkunden]. [Verein für geschichte des Bodensees und seiner umgebung: Schriften (nos.23–30): anhang:] Lindau 1894–1901. pp.vii.572. [1716.]

Bonde, family of.

JOHANNES FREDERICUS BAHR, Conspectus diplomatum in archivo illustr. familiáe Bondeanae in

Bourbon, house of.

[JEAN LOUIS ALPHONSE] HUILLARD-BRÉHOLLES, Titres de la maison ducale de Bourbon. Archives de l'empire: Inventaires et documents: 1867–1874 [–1882]. pp.[iv].iv–xliv.616 + [iii].vii.536.98. [8173.]

Bouret, family of.

EUGÈNE LE ROY, Inventaire sommaire des papiers et généalogie de la famille Bouret, de Gaulejac, près Montignac. Bergerac [printed] 1904. pp.76. [200.]

Family Names

Bousies de Rouveroy, family of.

RENÉE DOEHAERD, Inventaire des archives de la famille de Bousies de Rouveroy. Archives de l'état à Mons: Gembloux 1956. pp.51. [large number.]

Boyle, family of.

EDWARD MAC LYSAGHT, Calendar of the Orrery papers. Coimisiún láimhscríbhinní na hÉreann: Dublin 1941. pp.xi.396. [750.]

Brants, family of.

I[SABELLE] H[ENRIETTE] VAN EEGHEN, Inventaris van het familie-archief Brants. Gemeentelijke archiefdienst: Amsterdam 1959. pp.232. [10,000.]

Brien, family of.

BUELL-BRIEN papers. Tennessee state library and archives: Registers (no.7): Nashville 1964. pp. [v].21. [10,000.]*

Buell, family of.

BUELL-BRIEN papers. Tennessee state library and archives: Registers (no.7): Nashville 1964. pp. [v].21. [10,000.]*

Family Names

Butler, family of

EDMUND CURTIS, Calendar of Ormond deeds. Coimisún láimhscríbhinní na hÉireann: Dublin.
    [i]. 1172–1350. 1932. pp.lxiii.424. [863.]
    ii. 1350–1413. 1934. pp.xli.403. [442.]

Cadaval, family of.

VIRGÍNIA [ROBERTS] RAU and MARIA FERNANDA GOMES DA SILVA, Os manuscritos do arquivo da casa de Cadaval respeitantes ao Brasil. Acta universitatis conimbrigensis: [Coimbra] 1955–1958. pp.xv.543+[iii].483. [1118.]

Capizucchi, family of.

CONSTANTINO GIGLI, Catalogo overo indice di scrittori et istoriografi autorevoli, ne' cui libri et istorie stampate si fà onorevol mentione della nobil famiglia Capizucchi. Roma 1660. pp.61. [200.]

Champollion, family of.

[JEAN JACQUES] CHAMPOLLION-FIGEAC, Notice sur les manuscrits autographes de Champollion le jeune, perdus en l'année 1832 et retrouvés en 1840. 1842. pp.47. [13.]

Family Names

[HENRI JOSEPH] ADOLPHE ROCHAS, Notices biographiques et littéraires sur Champollion le jeune et mm. Champollion-Figeac. 1856. pp.17. [75.]

Coke, family of.

[WILLIAM DASHWOOD FANE], The manuscripts of the earl Cowper. Twelfth report of the Royal commission on historical manuscripts appendixes i–iii): 1888–1889. pp.vii.488+[ii].458+vi.329. [5000.]

Cole, family of.

ELMO R. RICHARDSON, The papers of Cornelius Cole and the Cole family, 1833–1943. A guide to collection 217. University of California: UCLA library occasional papers (no.4): Los Angeles 1956. ff.[viii].52. [large number.]★

Cornets de Groot, family of.

D. J. H. TER HORST, Overzicht van het familiearchief Cornets de Groot. Nationale bibliotheek: 's-Gravenhage 1940. pp.20. [10,000.]

Crillon, family of.

JEAN CORDEY [and A. BOUTILLIER DU RETAIL],

Inventaire des archives des ducs de Crillon conservées chez m. le marquis de Grammont. 1908. pp.ix.309. [1250.]

Croy, family of.

[LOUIS PROSPER] GACHARD, Notice des archives de m. le duc de Caraman. Bruxelles 1845. pp.[iv].148. [1000.]

Deering, family of.

ABSTRACTS of english records gathered principally in Devonshire and Essex in a search for the ancestry of Roger Dearing . . . and Matthew Whipple. Boston, Mass. 1929. pp.[xii].637. [Deering: 2000.]

150 copies privately printed.

De Hoghton, family of.

J. H. LUMBY, A calendar of the deeds and papers in the possession of sir James de Hoghton, bart., of Hoghton tower, Lancashire. Record society for the publication of original documents relating to Lancashire and Cheshire (vol.lxxxviii): 1936. pp.[vi].vi.372. [2000.]

Domville, family of.

ERIC A. BARKER, Talbot deeds, 1200–1682.

Record society for the publication of original documents relating to Lancashire and Cheshire (vol.ciii): Preston 1953. pp.[vii].89. [263.]

Douglas, family of.

[SIR WILLIAM FRASER (vol.ii: WILLIAM SCOTT)], The manuscripts [vol.ii: Report on the manuscripts] of his grace the duke of Buccleuch and Queensberry... preserved at Drumlanrig castle. Royal commission on historical manuscripts: 1897–1903. pp.[iii].334+[iii].243. [750.]
vol.i forms appendix vii to the Fifteenth report of the Royal commission.

Douxchamps, family of.

D. D. BROUWERS, Inventaire sommaire des archives de la famille Douxchamps déposées aux archives de l'état à Namur. [Brussels *c.*1910]. pp.7. [500.]

Du Coëtlosquet, family of.

RENÉ [M. M. P. DU COSQUER DE] KERVILER, Essai d'une bio-bibliographie de la famille Du Coëtlosquet. Vannes 1897. pp.31. [500.]

Family Names

Fanzago, family of.

[FRANCESCO FANZAGO], Bibliografia dei Fanzago. Padova 1902. pp.3–43. [148.]

Farrer, family of.

THOMAS CECIL, BARON FARRER OF ABINGER, Farrer wills and administrations . . . in England and Wales and the isle of Man down to A.D. 1880. Dorking [1936]. pp.425. [1700.]

— — Index . . . by Fredet Podmore. 1951. pp.220.

Fedorowicz, family of.

JEAN EM. LEWICKI [IVAN EMILIANOVICH LEVITSKY], Bibliographie des Fedorowicz. Léopol 1910. pp.[iii].232. [6000.]

Finch, family of.

[SOPHIE CRAWFORD LOMAS], Report on the manuscripts of Allan George Finch. Royal commission on historical manuscripts: 1913–1957. pp. lv.614+xxii.636+lviii.522. [4000.]

Folleville, family of.

[ADOLPHE ANDRÉ] PORÉE, Les archives du château de Folleville (Eure). 1902. pp.28. [62.]

Family Names

Forbin, family of.

J. H. ALBANÈS, Inventaire analytique des titres de la maison de Forbin. Marseille 1900. pp.[iii].v.297. [1396.]

Förstemann, family of.

ERNST WILHELM FÖRSTEMANN, Bibliographie der familie Förstemann. Leipzig 1906. pp.iv.50. [600.]

Foudras, family of.

F[RANÇOIS] M[ARIE] GUSTAVE MILLOT, Inventaire des archives de la maison de Foudras. Chalon-sur-Saône 1906. pp.10. [94.]

Fourneau de Cruquembourg, family of.

E. LEJOUR, Inventaire des archives de la famille de Fourneau de Cruquembourg. Archives générales du royaume: Bruxelles 1949. pp.78. [large number.]

Fugger, family of.

[FRANZ ANTON VEITH], De insignibvs illvstrissimae s. r. i. comitvm Fvggerorvm gentis in rem litterariam meritis libellvs singvlaris. [Augsburg 1790]. pp.[iv].92. [100.]

Family Names

Gaiffier, family of.

FERDINAND COURTOY, Inventaire des archives de la famille de Gaiffier-de Lévignen. Archives de l'état à Namur: Bruxelles 1949. pp.127. [large number.]

Gape, family of.

J. VACY LYLE, Report on the muniments of the Gape family, now deposited at the Hertfordshire county museum. St. Albans and Hertfordshire architectural and archæological society. St. Albans 1905. pp.34. [245.]

Gawdy, family of.

[WALTER RYE], Report on the manuscripts of the family of Gawdy, formerly of Norfolk. Tenth report of the Royal commission o historical manuscripts [appendix ii]: 1885. pp.iv.240. [1222.]

Gobart, family of.

E. LEJOUR, Inventaire des archives de la famille Gobart. Archives générales du royaume: Inventaires des archives de la Belgique: Tongres 1935. pp.99. [5000.]

Family Names

Gresley, family of.

ISAAC HERBERT JEAYES, Descriptive catalogue of the charters & muniments of the Gresley family in the possession of sir Robert Gresley, bart., at Drakelowe. 1895. pp.xiii.141. [1000.]

Grimaldi, family of.

[ALEXANDER BEAUFORT GRIMALDI], A catalogue, chronologically arranged, of printed books, pamphlets, articles, reviews, letters, poems, music, & memoranda, composed, edited, or translated, by writers bearing the name of Grimaldi. From 1498 to 1883. 1883. pp.127. [1167.]
100 copies privately printed.

Grimaldi-Regusse, family of.

G[ÉRAUD] LAVERGNE, Archives de la famille Grimaldi-Regusse. Inventaire. Monaco &c. 1911. pp.xii.323. [20,000.]

Grimm, family of.

HANS DAFFIS, Inventar der Grimm-schränke in der Preussischen staatsbibliothek. Preussische staatsbibliothek [Berlin]: Mitteilungen (vol.v): Leipzig 1923. pp.119. [2500.]

Family Names

Guicciardini, family of.

ROBERTO RIDOLFI, L'archivio della famiglia Guicciardini. Edizione riveduta e ampliata. Firenze 1931. pp.vii.150. [5000.]

the original edition appeared in vols.xxx–xxxii (1928–1930) of La bibliofilia.

Guise, family of.

[JEAN NICOLAS BEAUPRÉ], Notices analytiques de quelques écrits à consulter pour l'histoire de Lorraine au XVIe et au XVIIe siècle et pour l'histoire particulière de la maison de Guise. Saint-Nicolas-de-Port [printed] 1846. pp.24.

25 copies privately printed.

Guizot, family of.

J[OSEPH] M[ARIE] QUÉRARD, La famille Guizot. Monographie bibliographique. 1857. pp.32. [200.]

[H. GUÉRIN], Catalogues des ouvrages de Guizot (Éliza [Marguerite-Andrée-Éliza] Dillon, m^{me}), Guizot (François-Pierre-Guillaume), Guizot (Guillaume [Maurice-Guillaume]), Guizot (Jean-Jacques), Guizot (Pauline [Élisabeth-Charlotte-Pauline] de Meulan, m^{me}) conservés au département des imprimés. Bibliothèque nationale: 1917. pp.[ii].coll.70. [700.]

Family Names

Habsburg, family of.

CONSTANT WURZBACH VON TANNENBERG, Habsburg und Habsburg-Lothringen. Eine bibliobiographisch-genealogische studie. Wien 1861. pp.viii.505. [5000.]

JÁNOS KERTÉSZ, A Habsburg irodalom bibliographiája 1218–1934. Budapest 1934. pp.viii.coll. 192. [3000.]

— — [another issue]. Bibliographie der Habsburg-literatur. 1934. pp.vii.coll.192. [3000.]

Haller, family of.

[HEINZ ZIRNBAUER and BARON HELMUT HALLER VON HALLERSTEIN], Die Haller von Hallerstein. Stadtbibliothek: Ausstellungskatalog (no.21): Nürnberg [1961]. pp.[20]. [196.]

Halley, family of.

E. F. MAC PIKE, A short bibliography of the Halley families in Great Britain and America. San Diego, Cal. 1938. ff.[10]. [290.]*

Harley, family of.

THE MANUSCRIPTS of his grace the duke of Portland. Royal commission on historical manuscripts.

Family Names

i. [By F. H. Blackburne Daniell, Richard Ward and J. J. Cartwright]. 1891. pp. xxviii.723. [2000.]
ii. 1893. pp.xii.468. [1500.]
iii. 1894. pp.xiii.647. [2000.]
iv. 1897. pp.xx.705. [2000.]
v. 1899. pp.xv.677. [1250.]
vi. 1901. pp.viii.419. [250.]
vii. 1901. pp.xxv.531. [500.]
viii. 1907. pp.xxiv.432. [1000.]
ix. 1923. pp.x.434. [400.]
x. Edited by R. F. Isaacson. 1931. pp.vii.551. [750.]

vols.i–iv form respectively appendixes i and ii to the Thirteenth report, appendix ii to the Fourteenth report, and appendix iv to the Fifteenth report of the Royal commission.

Harmon, family of.

ROBERT B. HARMON, A preliminary checklist of materials on Harman–Harmon genealogy. San Jose, Cal. 1964. ff.iii.4.★

Hastings, family of.

[JOHN HARLEY and FRANCIS BICKLEY; vols.ii–iv: F. BICKLEY], Report on the manuscripts of the late

Reginald Rawdon Hastings. Royal commission on historical manuscripts: 1928–1947. pp.xviii.545 +xix.457+xvi.435+liii.463. [4000.]

Hausen, family of.

COUNT EBERHARD ZEPPELIN, Urkunden-regesten aus dem gräflich Douglas'schen archiv zu schloss Langenstein im Hegau. [Schriften des Vereins für geschichte des Bodensees und seiner umgebung (nos.18–19): anhang)]: Lindau 1889–1890. pp.76. [500.]

Hawkins, family of.

FRANCIS W[ILLIAM] STEER, The Hawkins papers. A catalogue. West Sussex county council: Chichester 1962. pp.vii.36. [2500.]

Herries, family of.

[SIR WILLIAM FRASER], Inventories of the muniments of the families of Maxwell, Herries and Nithsdale in the charter-room at Terregles. Edinburgh 1865. pp.viii.360. [Herries: 681.]

Heshuysen, family of.

I[SABELLE] H[ENRIETTE] VAN EEGHEN, Inventarissen van de familie-archieven Heshuysen, Hooft,

Hooft van Woudenberg. Gemeentelijke archiefdienst: Amsterdam 1960. pp.107. [25,000.]

Hirzel, family of.

ARCHIV der familie Hirzel. Handschriftenkatalog der stadtbibliothek Zürich (1. Abteilung, 1. Heft): Zürich 1907. pp.[iii].vii.76. [2500.]

Home, family of.

[WILLIAM FRASER], The manuscripts of the duke of Athole, K.T., and the earl of Home. Twelfth report of the Royal commission on historical manuscripts (appendix viii): 1891. pp.[iii].233. [Home: 500.]

Home of Wedderburn, family of.

[HENRY PATON], Report on the manuscripts of colonel David Milne Home. Royal commission on historical manuscripts: 1902. pp.[ii].329. [645.]

Hooft, family of.

I[SABELLE] H[ENRIETTE] VAN EEGHEN, Inventarissen van de familie-archieven Heshuysen, Hooft, Hooft van Woudenberg. Gemeentelijke archiefdienst: Amsterdam 1960. pp.107. [25,000.]

Family Names

Howard, family of.

[J. A. BENNETT and R. E. G. KIRK], The manuscripts of the earl of Carlisle. Fifteenth report of the Royal commission on historical manuscripts (appendix vi): 1897. pp.[iii].xxxviii.835. [1500.]

Huygens, family of.

[W. P. VAN STOCKUM *and others*], Catalogus van de tentoonstelling ter herinnering aan den 300-jarigen geboortedag van Constantijn Huygens. 's-Gravenhage 1896. pp.xii.146. [1000.]

Innes, family of.

SIR THOMAS INNES, Inventory of the principal progress-writs of the barony of Innes. Scottish record society (part 153): Edinburgh 1948. pp.[ii].59. [489.]

Jacopssen, family of.

JOS. MARÉCHAL, Inventaris van het archief der familie Jacopssen. Rijksarchief te Gent: Brussel 1949. pp.vi.37. [10,000.]

Kenyon, family of.

[WILLIAM JOHN HARDY], The manuscripts of lord

Kenyon. Fourteenth report of the Royal commission on historical manuscripts (appendix iv): 1894. pp.xi.706. [1450.]

Kerchove, family of.

ROBERT SCHOORMAN, Inventaire sommaire des archives de famille déposées aux archives de l'état, à Gand, par m. Arnold de Kerchove d'Ousselgem. [Brussels c.1910]. pp.5. [100.]

ROBERT SCHOORMAN, Inventaire sommaire des archives de la famille de Kerchove... déposées au dépôt des archives de l'état, à Gand, par le baron de Kerchove d'Exaerde. [Brussels c.1910]. pp.7. [200.]

ROBERT SCHOORMAN, Inventaire sommaire des archives de la famille de Kerchove... déposées au dépôt des archives de l'état, à Gand, par Astère de Kerchove de Dentergem. [Brussels c.1910]. pp.13. [1000.]

Kethulle, family of.

ROBERT SCHOORMAN, Inventaire sommaire des archives données à l'état par la famille de la Kethulle de Ryhove et déposées aux archives de l'état, à Gand. [Brussels c.1910]. pp.21. [1000.]

Family Names

Khevenhüller, family of.

GEORG KHEVENHÜLLER, Das landskroner archiv. Österreichische urkunden im schloss Thurnau in Oberfranken. Archiv für vaterländische geschichte und topographie (vol.55): Klagenfurt 1959. pp. 153. [5000.]

Lamont, family of.

SIR NORMAND LAMONT, An inventory of Lamont papers (1231–1897) . . . presented to the Scottish record society. Edinburgh [printed] 1914. pp.xi. 422. [1439.]

La Poype-Serrières, family of.

COUNT FRANÇOIS DE LA POYPE DE SERRIÈRES, Inventaire sommaire des anciennes archives de la maison de La Poype-Serrières, dressé postérieurement à 1741. . . . Publié d'après les manuscrits originaux, entièrement inédits, par [Jacques Paulze d'Ivoy de La Poype]. Grenoble 1888. pp.xi.241. [920.]

La Rousse de Pélacot, family of.

COMTE AMÉDÉE [DE SUREL SAINT-JULIEN] DE SAINT-AHOND, L'inventaire des preuves de noblesse de la maison de La Rousse de Pélacot. Surel [1901]. pp.24. [10.]

La Taille, family of.

J[OSEPH] DE LA TAILLE, Essai de bibliographie pour servir à l'histoire de la maison de La Taille. Besançon 1916. pp.43. [15.]

La Tour d'Auvergne, family of.

ALEXANDRE BRUEL, Inventaire d'une partie des titres de famille et documents historiques de la maison de La Tour d'Auvergne conservés dans les papiers Bouillon aux Archives nationales, pour faire suite aux inventaires rédigés par Baluze. Nogent-le-Rotrou [printed] 1900. pp.60. [650.]

La Trémoïlle, family of.

CHARLES [MAXIME DONATIEN] SAMARAN, Archives de la maison de La Trémoïlle (chartriers de Thouars et de Serrant, papiers Duchatel). Inventaires d'archives privées conservées en France (vol.i): 1928. pp.iii–xx.375. [50,000.]

Legh, family of.

F[RANK] TAYLOR, Hand-list of the Legh of

Family Names

Booths charters in the John Rylands library. Manchester 1950. pp.[ii].229–300. [362.]

Le Neve, family of.

FRANCIS and AMYRYE, Calendar of correspondence and documents relating to the family of Oliver Le Neve, of Witchingham, Norfolk, 1675–1743. Norwich 1895. pp.[ii].xxi.222. [2296.]

Lévignen, family of.

FERDINAND COURTOY, Inventaire des archives de famille de Gaiffier–de Lévignen. Archives de l'état à Namur: Bruxelles 1949. pp.127. [large number.]

Lévis, family of.

[SIMÉON OLIVE (vol.v: and F[ÉLIX] PASQUIER)] Archives du château de Léran. Inventaire historique et généalogique des documents de la branche Lévis-Léran devenue Lévis-Mirepoix [vol.iv: documents des branches latérales de la maison de Lévis]. Toulouse 1903–1927. pp.[iii].viii.484+[iii].556+660+[iii].725+xliii.754. [10,000.]

Lindsay, family of.

HENRY TENNYSON FOLKARD, A Lindsay record:

being a handlist of books written by or relating to members of the clan Lindsay: preserved in the Reference department of the Wigan free public library. Wigan [printed] 1899. pp.[v].45. [250.]
25 copies printed.

Lowther, family of.

[J. J. CARTWRIGHT], The manuscripts of the earl of Lonsdale. Thirteenth report of the royal commission on historical manuscripts (appendix vii): 1893. pp.viii.298. [200.]

Lyttelton, family of.

ISAAC HERBERT JEAYES, Descriptive catalogue of the charters & muniments of the Lyttelton family in the possession of... viscount Cobham. 1893. pp.xvi.154. [461.]

McIver, family of.

MCIVER collection. Tennessee state library and archives: Registers (no.4): Nashville 1962. pp. [v].9. [2000.]*

MacKaye, family of.

EDWIN OSGOOD GOVER, Annals of an era. Percy

Family Names

Mackaye [sic] and the Mackaye family, 1826–1932. A record of biography and history in commentaries and bibliography. Dartmouth college: Washington 1932. pp.[ii].xxiii.534.xlv–lxxix. [5000.]

McPike, family of.

E[UGENE] F[AIRFIELD] MACPIKE, Bibliographical references to the families of Pike, Pyke, MacPike, McPike in Great Britain and America. San Diego 1938. ff.[11]. [100.]*

Manners, family of.

[SIR HENRY CHURCHILL MAXWELL LYTE], The manuscripts of his grace the duke of Rutland. Royal commission on historical manuscripts: 1888–1905. pp.xxi.527+viii.496+xii.465+xii.675. [20,000.]

the first three volumes form appendixes iv and v to the Twelfth report and appendix i to the Fourteenth report of the Royal commission.

Mansell, family of.

[SIR THOMAS PHILLIPPS], Mansell records. [Middle Hill *n.d.*]. pp.[12]. [500.]

Family Names

Manuzio, family of.

ESTER PASTORELLO, L'epistolario manuziano. Inventario cronologico-analitico 1483-1597. Biblioteca di bibliografia italiana (vol.xxx): Firenze 1957. pp.351. [2401.]

also issued as Civiltà veneziana: Studi (no.3).

Mar, family of.

[HENRY PATON], Report on the manuscripts of the earl of Mar and Kellie. Royal commission on historical manuscripts: 1904. pp.xxviii.608. [1500.]

—— Supplementary report. 1930. pp.xiv.334. [750.]

Maurice, family of.

T. JONES PIERCE, Clenennau letters and papers in the Brogyntyn collection. Cylchgrawn llyfrgell genedlaethol Cymru: Atodiad (4th ser.): [Aberystwyth] 1947– . [643.]

Maxwell, family of.

[SIR WILLIAM FRASER], Inventories of the muniments of the families of Maxwell, Herries and Nithsdale in the charter-room at Terregles. Edinburgh 1865. pp.viii.360. [Maxwell: 854.]

pages 1–136, relating to the Maxwell family, were also issued separately.

Medici, family of.

[DOMENICO MORENI], Serie d'autori di opere risguardanti la celebre famiglia Medici. Firenze 1826. pp.xvi.392. [1200.]

Meerman, family of.

J[OHANNES] H[ERMAN] KERNKAMP, Inventaris der familiepapieren Meerman, van Westreenen, Dierkens en van Damme aanwezig in het Museum Meermanno - Westreenianum. 's-Gravenhage 1948. pp.80. [17,500.]

Meldeman, family of.

CÉCILE LEFÈVRE, Inventaire des archives de la famille de Meldeman de Bouré. Archives de l'état à Namur: Bruxelles 1953. pp.xi.35. [229.]

Mesdach, family of.

ROBERT SCHOORMAN, Inventaire sommaire des archives de la famille Mesdach . . . déposées au dépôt des archives de l'état, à Gand. [Brussels *c.*1910]. pp.5. [100.]

Family Names

Michel de Pierredon, count Marie Henri Thierry.

[COUNT M. H. T. MICHEL DE PIERREDON], Inventaire raisonné des titres produits pour les preuves de noblesse paternelle et maternelle faites par le c^{te} Marie-Henry-Thierry Michel de Pierredon. 1915. pp.40. [193.]

Mitford, family of.

FRANCIS W[ILLIAM] STEER, The Mitford archives. A catalogue. West Sussex county council: Chichester 1961. pp.xi.84. [1260.]

Moens, family of.

I[SABELLE] H[ENRIETTE] VAN EEGHEN, Inventaris van het familie-archief Moens (behorend tot het archief van het r. k. Jongenweeshuis). [The Hague] 1955. pp.62. [370.]

Monnard, family of.

CHARLES ROTH, Inventaire sommaire des fonds Monnard-Ceresolle. Bibliothèque cantonale et universitaire: Inventaires des fonds manuscrits (no.i): Lausanne 1957. ff.20. [2000.]*

Family Names

Montagu, family of.

[SOPHIE CRAWFORD LOMAS], Report on the manuscripts of lord Montagu of Beaulieu. Royal commission on historical manuscripts: 1900. pp. xviii.251. [500.]

Moore, family of.

A LIST of books in the Library of Congress on the Moore and Patten families. Library of Congress: Washington 1936. ff.4. [36.]*

Moore, family of, of Bankhall.

J. BROWNBILL, A calendar of the collection of deeds and papers of the Moore family of Bankhall co. Lanc., now in the Liverpool public library.... With ... a calendar of a further portion of the same collection, now in the university of Liverpool school of local history and records, by Kathleen Walker. Record society for the publication of original documents relating to Lancashire and Cheshire (vol.lxvii): Edinburgh [printed] 1913. pp.xv.281. [1484.]

Muhlenberg, family of.

FELIX REICHMANN, The Muhlenberg family. A bibliography compiled from the subject union

Family Names

catalog, Americana-Germanica of the Carl Schurz memorial foundation. Bibliographies on german american history (no.1): Philadelphia 1943. pp.43. [400.]*

Neve, family of.

ROBERT SCHOORMAN, Inventaire sommaire des archives de la famille de Neve de Roden . . . déposées au dépôt des archives de l'état, à Gand. [Brussels *c.*1910]. pp.13. [1000.]

Nithsdale, family of.

[SIR WILLIAM FRASER], Inventories of the muniments of the families of Maxwell, Herries and Nithsdale in the charter-room at Terregles. Edinburgh 1865. pp.viii.360. [Nithsdale: 289.]

Noailles, family of.

[ANTOINE] LOUIS PARIS, Les papiers de Noailles de la bibliothèque du Louvre. Dépouillement de toutes les pièces qui composaient cette précieuse collection brulée. 1875. pp.[iii].iii.xxiv.324+[v]. vii.176. [2500.]

Norris, family of.

J. H. LUMBY, A calendar of the Norfolk deeds

(Lancashire) 12th to 15th century. Record society for the publication of original documents relating to Lancashire and Cheshire (vol.xciii): [*s.l.*] 1939. pp.[vi].vii.289. [1172.]

Olmen de Poederlé, family of.

MARIE ROSE THIELEMANS, Inventaire des archives de la famille d'Olmen de Poederlé. Archives de l'état à Mons: Bruxelles 1959. pp.xxi.149. [5000.]

Orange, house of.

CATALOGUS der tentoonstelling van voorwerpen betrekking hebbende op het vorstelijk stamhuis Oranje-Nassau. 's Gravenhage 1880. pp.viii.472. [3100.]

Ormesson, family of.

MICHEL ANTOINE and YVONNE LANHERS, Les archives d'Ormesson. Archives nationales: 1960. pp.3–123. [20,000.]

Ormonde, family of.

[SIR JOHN THOMAS and ROSA GILBERT], The manuscripts [vol.ii: Report on the manuscripts] of the marquis of Ormonde. Royal commission

Family Names

on historical manuscripts: 1895–1899. pp.viii.455
+vi.491. [800.]

*the first volume forms appendix vii to the Fourteenth
report of the Royal commission.*

—— Index. [By S. C. Ratcliff]. 1909. pp.[v].
227.

—— Calendar of the manuscripts of the marquess of Ormonde. . . . New series. [By C. Litton Falkiner and F. Elrington Ball]. 1902–1920. pp. xii.360 + xix.428 + xx.480 + xxiv.724 + xvi.669+xxii.607+xx.591+lv.460. [4000.]

Pakington, family of.

CALENDAR of the Hampton collection of manuscripts, being documents relating to the Pakington family and estates in the counties of Worcester, Buckingham and Pembroke, and elsewhere, compiled from the originals deposited on permanent loan in the Birmingham reference library by the rt. hon. Herbert Stuart Pakington, D.S.O., 4th baron Hampton. [Birmingham] 1941. ff.[i].iii.543. [3000.]*

Parry, family of.

G. S. PARRY, Genealogical abstracts of Parry wills proved in the Prerogative court of Canterbury down to 1810, with the administrations for the same period. 1911. pp.[iv].152. [689.]

Perceval, family of.

[SOPHIE CRAWFORD LOMAS, WILLIAM PAGE and RICHARD ARTHUR ROBERTS], Report on the manuscripts of the earl of Egmont. Royal commission on historical manuscripts: 1905–1923. pp.lxxii.336 + [ii].337–758 + xviii.271 + xix.477 + vi.517 + xii.542. [2500.]
the last three volumes consist of the diary of the first earl of Egmont.

Pike, family of.

E. F. MAC PIKE, Bibliographical references to the families of Pike, Pyke, MacPike, McPike in Great Britain and America. San Diego 1938. ff.[11]. [100.]*

Potocki, family of.

WŁADISŁAW SEMKOWICZ and PIOTR BAŃKOWSKI, Przewodnik po zbiorze rękopisów wilanowskich. Warszaw 1961. pp.viii.368. [1000.]

Praet, family of.

BARON A. VAN ZUYLEN VAN NYEVELT, Inventaire

sommaire des archives de la baronne de Praet et de la paroisse d'Oedelem conservées au dépôt des archives de l'état, à Bruges. [Brussels c.1910]. pp.8. [446.]

Preston, family of.

JAMES MILLS and M. J. MCENERY, Calendar of the Gormanston register. Royal society of antiquaries of Ireland (extra volume): Dublin 1916. pp.[ii]. xx.252. [1000.]

Preudhomme, family of.

J. BUNTINX, Inventaris van het archief der familie de Preudhomme d'Hailly en der aanverwante families. Rijksarchief te Gent: Brussel 1950. pp.98. [834.]

Pudsay, family of.

RALPH PUDSAY LITTLEDALE, The Pudsay deeds. The Pudsays of Bolton and Barforth, and their predecessors in those manors. Yorkshire archæological society: Record series (vol.lvi): [s.l.] 1916. pp.vii.434. [481.]

Radoliński, family of.

STANISLAUS [STANISŁAW] KARWOWSKI, Catalogus

Family Names

archivi Radolinsciani jarocinensis. Posnaniae 1911. pp.173. [3000.]

Rathbone, family of.

[D. F. COOK], Catalogue of the Rathbone papers in the university library. [Liverpool] 1959. pp.vi.26+iii.3. [large number.]*

Rechteren, family of.

D[IRK] P[ETRUS] M[ARIUS] GRASWINCKEL and H. HARDENBERG, Het archief van het Kasteel Rechteren. 's-Gravenhage 1941. pp.lx.540. [683.] *extends to 1588.*

Reede, family of van.

[P. BERENDS], Inventaris van stukken betreffende ambten en waardigheden bekleed door leden van het geslacht van Reede (van Athlone). [s.l. 1901]. pp.[iv].v.68. [716.]

Reinach, family of.

MATHIEU MÉRAS [*and others*], Les archives de la famille de Reinach. Archives départementales du Haut-Rhin: Colmar 1961. pp.3–471. [5000.]

Richmond, family of.

HENRY I. RICHMOND, Richmond family records.

Family Names

   i. Maryland, Virginia, New England, Ireland and Somerset. 1933. pp.viii.232. [1000.]
   ii. The Richmonds alias Webb of Wiltshire. 1935. pp.xv.269. [1250.]
   iii. The Richmonds of Wiltshire. 1938. pp. xvi.327. [1500.]
no more published.

Ridgely, family of.

LEON DEVALINGER and VIRGINIA E. SHAW, A calendar of Ridgely family letters, 1742–1899, in the Delaware state archives. Dover 1948–1951. pp.349.36+344.37. [2000.]

Robespierre, family of.

J[OSEPH] M[ARIE] QUÉRARD, Les Robespierre. Monographie bibliographique. 1863. pp.44. [330.]
  100 copies printed.

Romanov, house of.

[S. GORYAINOV], 'Дѣла собственно до Императорской Фамиліи относящіяся'. Министерство иностранныхъ дѣлъ: Государственный архивъ (series II): С.-Петербургъ 1913. pp.iv.118.66. [1825.]

Family Names

Rosenberg, family of.

JOSEF PELIKÁN, Rožmberské dluhopisy z let 1457–1481. Československa akademie věd: Studie a prameny k Českym dějinám (vol.4): Praha 1953. pp.xv.292. [680.]

Rosecrans, family of.

JAMES V. MINK, The papers of general William Starke Rosecrans and the Rosecrans family. University of California: UCLA library occasional paper (no.12): Los Angeles 1961. pp.ix.39. [large number.]*

Ryder, family of.

MICHAEL GEORGE BROCK, Harrowby mss. [1950 &c.]*

in progress; a catalogue of the manuscripts of John Herbert Dudley, earl of Harrowby.

Sackville, family of.

[R. B. KNOWLES and W. O. HEWLETT], The manuscripts of mrs. Stopford Sackville, of Drayton house, Northamptonshire. Ninth report of the Royal commission on historical manuscripts (part iii): 1884. pp.[ii].150. [1500.]

Family Names

— — [revised edition]. Report on the manuscripts of mrs. Stopford-Sackville. [By Sophie Crawford Lomas]. Royal commission on historical manuscripts: 1904–1910. pp.viii.439+vii.359. [2500.]

Salm, family of.

L. SCHMITZ[-KALLENBERG], Urkunden des fürstlich Salm-Salm'schen archives in Anhalt. Historische kommission der provinz Westfalen: Inventare der nichtstaatlichen archive (beiband i, heft i): Münster 1902. pp.[iv].242. [1173.]

Salusbury, family of.

W[ILLIAM] J[AMES] SMITH, Calendar of Salusbury correspondence, 1553–circa 1700, principally from the Lleweni, Rûg and Bagot collections in the National library of Wales. University of Wales: Board of celtic studies: History and law series (no.xiv): Cardiff 1954. pp.xvii.299. [554.]

Saluzzo, family of.

ARMANDO TALLONE, Regesto dei marchesi di Saluzzo (1091–1340). Società storica subalpina: Biblioteca (vol.xvi): Pinerolo 1906. pp.[iii].xviii.547. [1050.]

Family Names

Sanguszko, family of.

KATALOG rękopisów archiwum x.x. Sanguszków. Sławucie 1902. pp.[v].xlv.488. [5000.]

Sargent, family of.

JULIA MEHITABLE JOHNSON, A list of publications of the descendants of Epes Sargent. [s.l. 1923]. pp.68. [1250.]

Schaffgotsch, family of.

HEINRICH NENTWIG, Schaffgotschiana in der Reichsgräflich Schaffgotsch'schen majorats-bibliothek zu Warmbrunn. Leipzig 1899. pp.vii.64. [300.]

Schenk, family of.

KARL HANNAKAM and LUDWIG VEIT, Archiv der freiherrn Schenk von Geyern auf Schloss Syburg. Bayerische archivinventare (no.11): München 1958. pp.xvi.340. [large number.]

Secco, family of.

GIUSEPPE BONELLI, L'archivio Silvestri in Calcio. Notizia e inventario-regesto. Torino 1912. pp.

Family Names

[v].xii.123+[iv].xxi.121+[iv].xviii.171. [1655.]
300–350 copies printed.

Ségur, family of.

GRAF VICTOR SÉGUR-CABANAC, Bibliographie des gräflichen hauses Ségur, seine genealogischen beziehungen zu dem hause Lothringen. Wien 1911. pp.xvi.260. [200.]
300 copies printed.

Shiffner, family of.

FRANCIS W[ILLIAM] STEER, The Shiffner archives. A catalogue. East Sussex county council: Lewes 1959. pp.xvii.126. [3749.]

Sidney, family of.

[C. L. KINGSFORD (iii–iv: WILLIAM A. SHAW)], Report on the manuscripts of lord de L'Isle & Dudley. Royal commission on historical manuscripts: 1925–1942. pp.lx.550+xxxvii.732+lxxix.547+xxxii.375. [3300.]

    i–ii. 1925–1934. pp.lx.550 + xxxvii.732. [3000.]

    iv. Sidney papers, 1608–1611. 1942. pp.xxxii.395. [750.]

Family Names

v. Sidney papers, 1611–1626. 1962. pp.xliii. 488. [750.]
in progress?

Smallbrook, family of.

CALENDAR of deeds relating to estates of the Smallbrook family in Birmingham and . . . elsewhere. Reference library: Birmingham 1938. ff.[i].23. [175.]*

Spaen, van, family of.

SUZE M. VAN ZANTEN JUT, Inventaris van het familiearchief van Spaen. Hooge raad van adel: 's-Gravenhage 1953. pp.138. [2500.]

Standish, family of.

THOMAS CRUDDAS PORTEUS, Calendar of the Standish deeds, 1230–1575, . . . together with abstracts . . . of 228 deeds not now in the collection. Public libraries: Wigan 1933. pp.xiv.156. [469.]
250 copies printed.

— — Index . . . by Arthur John Hawkes. Public library: Wigan 1937. pp.xxxii.

Stella, family of.

GIUSEPPE BONELI, Un archivio privato del

cinquecento. Le carte Stella. Milano 1908. pp.57. [389.]

Strauss, family of.

CHR[ISTIAN] FLAMME, Verzeichnis der sämtlichen, im druck erschienenen kompositionen von Johann Strauss (vater), Johann Strauss (sohn), Josef Strauss und Eduard Strauss. Leipzig 1898. pp.90. [1250.]

ALEXANDER WEINMANN, Verzeichnis sämtlicher werke von Johann Strauss vater und sohn. Beiträge zur geschichte des alt-wiener musikverlages (1st ser., vol.2): Wien [1956]. pp.172. [1500.]

Stuart, house of.

[F. H. BLACKBURNE DANIELL], Calendar of the stuart papers belonging to his majesty the king. Royal commission on historical monuments: 1902 &c.

    i. 1902. pp.ciii.616. [750.]
    ii. 1904. pp.xlvi.614. [750.]
    iii. 1907. pp.xlvii.656. [750.]
    iv. 1910. pp.xlii.631. [750.]
    v. 1912. pp.xxviii.763. [900.]
    vi. 1916. pp.xc.842. [1000.]
    vii. 1923. pp.xxxviii.857. [1000.]

Family Names

FRANCIS JOHN ANGUS SKEET, Stuart papers, pictures, relics, medals and books in the collection of miss Maria Widdrington. Leeds 1930. pp.xi.98. [300.]
375 copies printed.

Stubenberg, family of.

JOH. LOSERTH, Das archiv des hauses Stubenberg. Historischer verein für Steiermark: Beiträge zur erforschung steirischer geschichte (vol.xxxv): Graz 1906. pp.198. [2500.]

Thézan, family of.

[EUTROPE FULESAN JOSEPH LOUIS MARIE PONS ROSTAING DE BADERON], MARQUIS DE THEZAN SAINT-GENIEZ, Le fonds Thézan aux archives du château de l'Hermitage (Hérault). . . . Inventaire des documents intéressant cette maison [by Henri Blaquière]. Montpellier [printed] 1938. pp.326. [large number.]

Tresham, family of.

[JOHN TAYLOR], A calendar of papers of the Tresham family, of the reigns of Elizabeth and James I, 1580–1605, preserved at Rushton hall,

Northamptonshire. Northampton 1871. pp.16. [200.]

Tronchin, family of.

FRÉD[ÉRIC] GARDY, Catalogue de la partie des archives Tronchin acquise par la Société du Musée historique de la Réformation. Genève 1946. pp. xvii.194. [4000.]

Van den Hecke, family of.

ROBERT SCHOORMAN, Inventaire sommaire des archives de la famille van den Hecke ... déposées aux archives de l'état, à Gand. [Brussels c.1910]. pp.15. [1000.]

Van der Bruggen, family of.

ROBERT SCHOORMAN, Inventaire sommaire des archives de la famille Van der Bruggen ... déposées aux archives de l'état, à Gand. [Brussels c.1910]. pp.8. [500.]

Van der Noot, family of.

E. LEJOUR, Inventaire des archives de la famille Van der Noot. Archives générales du royaume: Bruxelles 1954. pp.148. [5000.]

Family Names

Velasco, family of.

M[ARGARIT]A TERESA DE LA PEÑA MARAZUELA and PILAR LEÓN TELLO, Archivo de los duques de Frías. Inventario. Madrid 1955 &c.
in progress.

Veldenz, family of.

CARL PÖHLMANN, Regesten der lehensurkunden der grafen von Veldenz. Pfälzische gesellschaft zur förderung der wissenschaften: Veröffentlichungen (vol.iii): Speier 1928. pp.[iii].352. [738.]

Vezins, family of.

H[ENRI] BOUSQUET, Inventaire des archives du château de Vezins. Commission des archives historiques du Rouergue: Archives historiques du Rouergue (vol.xii, xiii, xv): Rodez 1934–1942. pp.661+477+534. [4999.]
300 copies printed.

Vigarini, family of.

GABRIEL ROUCHÈS, Inventaire des lettres et papiers manuscrits de Gaspare, Carlo et Lodovico Vigarini conservés aux Archives d'état de Modène (1634–1688). Société de l'histoire de l'art fran-

çais: Collection: 1913. pp.[vii].xxxvii.237. [390.]
also issued as a Paris thesis.

Ville, family of.

JULIETTE ROUHART-CHABOT, Inventaire de la famille de Monin et de la famille de Ville de Goyet. Archives de l'état à Namur: Bruxelles 1961. pp. [iii].137.19. [5000.]*

Vogüé, family of.

INVENTAIRE des archives du château de Vogüé fait en 1712. Publié . . . par le m^{is} de Vogüé. Sancerre [printed] 1905. pp.[v].152. [588.]

Well, family of.

A. F. VAN BEURDEN, Catalogus van het oud-archief van het kasteel en der baronie Well toebehoorende aan "de maatschappij Well". Roermond 1906. pp.88.

Welser, family of.

[HEINZ ZIRNBAUER and FRANZ XAVER PRÖLL], Die Welser. Stadtbibliothek: Ausstellungs-katalog (no.17): Nürnberg 1960. pp.[19]. [175.]

Family Names

Westreenen, family of van.

J[OHANNES] H[ERMAN] KERNKAMP, Inventaris der familiepapieren Meerman, van Westreenen, Dierkens en van Damme aanwezig in het Museum Meermanno-Westreenianum 's-Gravenhage 1948. pp.80. [17,500.]

Whipple, family of.

ABSTRACTS of english records gathered principally in Devonshire and Essex in a search for the ancestry of Roger Dearing . . . and Matthew Whipple. Boston, Mass. 1929. pp.[xii].637. [Whipple: 1000.]

150 copies privately printed.

White, family of.

MARGARET ELLS, A calendar of the White collection of manuscripts. Public archives of Nova Scotia: Publication (no.5): Halifax, N.S. 1940. pp.130.xi. [1561.]

Willoughby, family of.

[W. H. STEVENSON], Report on the manuscripts of lord Middleton. Royal commission on historical manuscripts: 1911. pp.xv.746. [1500.]

Family Names

Wittelsbach, family of.

GEORG LEIDINGER, Katalog der Wittelsbacherausstellung. Königliche hof- und staatsbibliothek. München 1911. pp.40. [573.]

Wolffskeel, family of.

MICHAEL RENNER and ERICH STAHLEDER, Archiv der grafen Wolffskeel von Reichenberg. Bayerische archivinventare (no.17): München 1961. pp.xv.131. [1200.]

Wynn, family of.

[MARJORIE FOLJAMBE HALL], Calendar of Wynn (of Gwydir) papers, 1515–1690, in the National library of Wales and elsewhere. Aberystwyth &c. 1926. pp.v–xx.512. [2873.]

Place Names

Bedfordshire.

F. A. BLAYDES, A calendar of some Bedfordshire wills, collected from various sources, relating chiefly to the gentry and clergy of the county of Bedford. Bedford 1893. pp.[85]. [1000.]

[F. G. EMMISON], Bedfordshire marriage licences (bonds and allegations for marriage licences, preserved in the Bedfordshire archdeaconry records). Bedfordshire parish registers (vol.xiv &c.): Bedford.

    i. 1747–1790 . . . (vol.xiv): 1937. pp.169. [2250.]

    ii. 1791–1812 . . . (vol.xv): 1937. pp.210. [3000.]

no more published; 100 copies reproduced from typewriting.

Berkshire.

W[ILLIAM] P[HILLIMORE] [WATTS] PHILLIMORE, Index to wills proved and administrations granted

Place Names

in the Court of the archdeacon of Berks, 1508 to 1652. British record society: Index library (vol.viii): 1893. pp.viii.199. [22,000.]

Boston, Mass.

[W. S. APPLETON], A report of the Record commissioners of the city of Boston, containing Boston births from A.D. 1700 to A.D. 1800. Boston 1894. pp.iv.379. [12,000.]

described on the cover as the 'Twenty-fourth report of the Record commissioners'.

[EDWARD WEBSTER MCGLENEN], A report of the Record commissioners of the city of Boston, containing the Boston marriages from 1700 to 1751 [1752 to 1890]. Boston 1898–1903. pp.viii.468 + vii.712. [27,500.]

described on the covers as the 'Twenty-eighth [Thirtieth] report of the Record commissioners'.

· [WILLIAM HENRY WHITMORE and WILLIAM S. APPLETON], A report of the Record commissioners containing Boston births, baptisms, marriages, and deaths, 1630–1699. Boston 1908. pp.vii.281. [10,000.]

described on the cover as the 'Ninth report of the Record commissioners'; the preface is dated 1883.

Place Names

Cambridge.

CALENDAR of wills proved in Vice-chancellor's court at Cambridge, 1501–1765. Cambridge 1907. pp.74. [1500.]

CAMBRIDGESHIRE parish registers. Marriages. Index to vols.I–VI. 1919. pp.vii.221. [30,000.]
100 copies printed.

Carolina, South.

INDEXES to the county wills of South Carolina ... compiled from the W.P.A. copies of each of the county will books except those of Charleston county ... in the ... university of South Carolina library. Columbia 1939. [large number.]*
the pagination is erratic.

Cheshire, Chester.

WILLIAM BEAMONT, Arley charters. A calendar of ancient family charters preserved at Arley hall, Cheshire, the seat of R. E. Egerton-Warburton. Newton [printed] 1866. pp.[ii].xlii.75. [600.]

BIBLIOGRAPHY of Lancashire and Cheshire. Publications issued in the two counties during 1876. Manchester 1877. pp.vii.38. [400.]

Place Names

J[OHN] P[ARSONS] EARWAKER [1760–1800: W(IL-LIA)M FERGUSSON IRVINE; 1801–1810: R(ONALD) STEWART-BROWN; 1821–1825: ROBERT DICKINSON], An index to the wills and inventories now preserved in the Court of probate at Chester. Record society for the publication of original documents relating to Lancashire and Cheshire (vol.ii &c.).

1545–1620 . . . (vol.ii): 1879. pp.xxxvi.224. [11,500.]

1621–1650 . . . (vol.iv): 1881. pp.xii.303. [15,000.]

1660–1680 . . . (vol.xv): 1887. pp.xii.380. [19,000.]

1681–1700 . . . (vol.xviii): 1888. pp.x.365. [18,000.]

1701–1720 . . . (vol.xx): 1889. pp.viii.261. [13,000.]

1721–1740 . . . (vol.xxii): 1890. pp.viii.343. (17,000.]

1741–1760 . . . (vol.xxv): 1892. pp.viii.264. [13,000.]

1761–1780 . . . (vol.xxxvii–xxxviii): 1898–1899. pp.[viii].200+[vi].123. [6000.]
on the titlepage of vol.xxxviii the dates wrongly appear as 1741–1760.

1781–1790 . . . (vol.xliv): 1902. pp.[vi].168. [8000.]

Place Names

    1791–1800 . . . (vol.xlv): 1902. pp.[vii].242. [12,000.]

    1801–1810 . . . (vols.lxii–lxiii): 1911–1912. pp.viii.245+viii.201. [15,000.]

    1811–1820 . . . (vols.lxxviii–lxxix):
        [*continued as:*]

An index to the wills and administrations formerly preserved in the probate registry, at Chester.

    1821–1825. . . . (vol.cvii): 1961. pp.vii.243. [9000.]

no records exist for the period 1651–1659.

W[ILLIA]M FERGUSSON IRVINE, Marriage licences granted within the archdeaconry of Chester in the diocese of Chester. Record society for the publication of original documents relating to Lancashire and Cheshire (vol.liii &c.).

    i. 1606–1616 . . . (vol.liii): 1907. pp.ix.255. [3500.]

    ii. 1616–1624 . . . (vol.lvi): 1908. pp.[v].257. [3500.]

    iii. 1624–1632 . . . (vol.lvii): 1909. pp.[v].308. [4000.]

    iv. 1639–1644 . . . (vol.lxi): 1911. pp.[iii].170. [2000.]

    v. 1661–1667 . . . (vol.lxv): 1921. pp.vi.284. [3000.]

Place Names

vi. 1667–1680 ... (vol.lxix): 1914. pp.vi.335. [4500.]

vii. 1680–1691 ... (vol.lxxiii): 1918. pp.vi.232. [3000.]

viii. 1691–1700 ... (vol.lxxvii): 1924. pp.viii.378. [2500.]

MARRIAGE bonds of the ancient archdeaconry of Chester now preserved at Chester. Record society for the publication of original documents relating to Lancashire and Cheshire (vol.lxxxii &c.).

i. 1700–1706–7. Edited by W[illia]m Asheton Tonge ... (vol.lxxxiii): 1933. pp.vi.302. [2000.]

ii. 1707–1711. Edited by W[illia]m Fergusson Irvine ... (vol.lxxxv): 1935. pp.[iv].271. [2000.]

iii. 1711–1715 ... (vol.xcvii): 1942. pp.[iv].185. [2000.]

iv. 1716–1719. Edited by P. H. Lawson ... (vol.ci): 1946. pp.[iv].333. [2500.]

in progress.

ROBERT DICKINSON, An index to the wills and administration formerly preserved in the probate registry at Chester for the years 1821–1825 both inclusive. Record society for the publication of original documents relating to Lancashire and

Place Names

Cheshire (vol.cvii): Blackpool 1961. pp.vii.243. [7000.]

Chichester.

EDWARD ALEXANDER FRY, Calendar of wills in the Consistory court of the bishop of Chichester, 1482–1800. British record society: Index library (vol.xlix): 1915. pp.viii.415. [22,500.]

EDW. ALEX. FRY, Calendar of administrations in the Consistory court of the bishop of Chichester, 1555–1800. Calendar of wills and administrations in the Peculiar court of the archbishop of Canterbury, 1520–1670. Calendar of wills and administrations in the Peculiar court of the dean of Chichester, 1577–1800. British record society: Index library (vol.lxiv): 1940. pp.xii.269. [13,000.]

Cork and Ross.

HERBERT WEBB GILLMAN, Index to the marriage licence bonds of the diocese of Cork and Ross, Ireland, for the years from 1623 to 1750. Public record office: Cork 1896–1897. pp.v.141. [12,500.]

Cornwall.

[THOMAS QUILLER COUCH and CHARLES CHORLEY], Bibliotheca cornubiensis. Preparatory lists.

Place Names

[Royal institution of Cornwall: Truro 1865]. pp. 69.[vii]. [1250.]

EDWA[RD] ALEX[ANDER] FRY, Calendars of wills and administrations relating to the counties of Devon and Cornwall, proved in the court of the principal registry of the bishop of Exeter, 1559–1799 . . . preserved in the probate registry at Exeter. Devonshire association for the advancement of science, literature, and art: Plymouth [1899–]1908[–1912]. pp.xxiii.878. [65,000.]

EDW[ARD] ALEX[ANDER] FRY, Calendars of wills and administrations relating to the counties of Devon and Cornwall, 1540–1799 [1532–1800]. British record society: Index library (vols.xxxv, xlvi): 1904, 1914. pp.xxiii.878+vi.324. [87,500.]

EDWARD ALEXANDER FRY, A calendar of inquisitiones post mortem for Cornwall and Devon, . . . 1216–1649. Devon and Cornwall record society: Exeter 1906 [1905]. pp.vii.185. [4500.]

A. TERRY SATTERFORD, Cornwall parish registers. Marriages. Index to vols.I–VI. 1915. pp.viii. 197. [30,000.]
100 copies printed.

R. M. GLENCROSS, Calendar of wills, administrations and accounts relating to the counties of

Place Names

Cornwall and Devon in the Connotorial archidiaconal court of Cornwall, 1569–1699 [–1799]. British record society: Index library (vols.lvi, lix): 1929, 1932. pp.vi.373+[v].243. [60,000.]

Devonshire.

EDWA[RD] ALEX[ANDER] FRY, Calendars of wills and administrations relating to the counties of Devon and Cornwall, proved in the court of the principal registry of the bishop of Exeter, 1559–1799, and of Devon only, proved in the court of the archdeaconry of Exeter, 1540–1799, all now preserved in the probate registry at Exeter. Devonshire association for the advancement of science, literature, and art: Plymouth [1899–]1908[–1912]. pp.xxiii.878. [65,000.]

EDW[ARD] ALEX[ANDER] FRY, Calendars of wills and administrations relating to the counties of Devon and Cornwall, 1540–1799 [1532–1800]. British record society: Index library (vols.xxxv, xlvi): 1904, 1914. pp.xxiii.878+vi.324. [87,500.]

ROGER GRANVILLE and W. E. MUGFORD, Abstracts of the existing transcript of the lost parish-registers of Devon, 1596–1644. . . . Volume I, A–Bra. Exeter 1908. pp.vii.192. [2500.]
no more published; 300 copies printed.

Place Names

CALENDAR of wills and administrations in the Consistory court of the bishop of Exeter, 1532 to 1800. Devonshire association for the advancement of literature, science, and art: Plymouth 1910–1912. pp.242. [25,000.]

R. M. GLENCROSS, Calendar of wills, administrations and accounts relating to the counties of Cornwall and Devon in the Connotorial archidiaconal court of Cornwall, 1569–1699 [–1799]. British record society: Index library (vols.lvi, lix): 1929, 1932. pp.vi.373+[v].243. [60,000.]

Dorsetshire.

EDWARD ALEXANDER FRY [vol.ii: GEORGE SAMUEL FRY], A calendar of wills and administrations relating to the county of Dorset . . . 1568– . . . 1799. British record society: Index library (vols.xxii, liii): 1900, 1922. pp.x.271+vii.184. [25,000.]

GEORGE S[AMUEL] FRY, Calendar of Dorset wills proved in the Prerogative court of Canterbury, Somerset house. Dorset records (vol.xi): 1911. pp.[iii].115. [6000.]
privately printed.

Ducklington.

W[ILLIAM] D[UNN] MACRAY, An index to the

Place Names

registers of baptism, marriages, and burials in the parish of Ducklington. North Oxfordshire archæological society: Transactions (1880): Oxford 1881. pp.viii.70. [7500.]

Durham.

[HERBERT M. WOOD], Index of wills, etc., in the probate registry, Durham, and from other sources, 1540–1599. Newcastle upon Tyne records committee: Publications (vol.viii): Newcastle 1928. pp.[ix].234. [5000.]

Exeter, city and diocese of.

J. L. VIVIAN, *ed*. The marriage licences of the diocese of Exeter. Exeter 1887. pp.120. [5500.]

— — Indices to Vivian's Exeter marriage licences, 1523–1631 . . . by S. Pershouse. [1948]. ff.182.*

THE MARRIAGE licences of the diocese of Exeter. [Edited by] John Henry Mann. Devon & Cornwall record society: [Exeter].*

    1631–1668. 1939. ff.[ii].ii.426. [6250.]
    1668–1704. 1941. ff.[ii].ii.322+[i].323–649+ [ii].325. [16,000.]
    1704–1734. 1942. ff.[ii].ii.320+[ii].320–607+ [ii].268. [15,000.]

Place Names

1734–1762. 1947. ff.[ii].iii.441+[i].441–858+
[ii].338. [21,000.]

MARRIAGE allegations, Devon and Cornwall. [Edited by] John Henry Mann. Devon & Cornwall record society: [Exeter].*
- i. 1660–1697.
- ii. 1700–1710.
- iii. 1711–1719.
- iv. 1720–1725.
- v. 1726.
- vi. 1727–1733–4. 1938. ff.[ii].218. [3000.]
- — Consolidated indexes ... 1660–1733. 1939. ff.[ii].ii.381.

Flintshire.

J. H. E. BENNETT and P. H. LAWSON, Index to the wills proved at the Peculiar court of Hawarden and to miscellaneous papers relating to the same court (now preserved at the St. Asaph court of probate) from 1554 to 1880. [Flintshire historical society: Publications (vol.iv)]: Prestatyn [printed] [1913]. pp.3–74. [2000.]

E[DWARD] R[HYS] HARRIES, Bibliography of the county of Flint. Flintshire county library: Mold.
 i. Biographical sources. 1953. pp.70. [3000.]
in progress.

121

Place Names

Forez.

A[UGUSTE] CHAVERONDIER, Notice sur le recueil des testaments enregistrés en la chancellerie du Forez, 1272–1467. Saint-Étienne 1888. pp.91. [250.]

Gloucester, city, county and diocese of.

[SIR THOMAS PHILLIPPS], Index of wills at Gloucester [1541–1555]. [Middle hill c.1840]. pp.20 [sic, 24]. [2500.]

Halberton.

A. W. WATERHOUSE, Index to Halberton register. Society of genealogists: 1937. ff.[i].96. [50,000.]*

Hampshire.

WILLIAM J[OHN] C[HARLES] MOENS, Hampshire allegations for marriage licences granted by the bishop of Winchester, 1689 to 1837. Publications of the Harleian Society (vols.xxxv–xxxvi): 1893. pp.vii.553+[iv].429. [25,000.]

Harrison county, Ohio.

CHARLES A. HANNA, Historical collections of Harrison county, in the state of Ohio. With lists of the first land-owners, early marriages (to 1841),

Place Names

will records (to 1861), burial records of the early settlements, and numerous genealogies. New York 1900. pp.viii.636. [15,000.]

Hertfordshire.

WILLIAM BRIGG, A calendar of wills and administrations. Archdeaconry of St. Albans. . . . Part I. Register 'Stonham', 1415–1470. Harpenden 1895. pp.[iii].25. [1250.]
no more published.

Huntingdonshire.

W. M. NOBLE, Calendars of Huntingdonshire wills, 1479–1652. British record society: Index library (vol.xlii): 1911. pp.xii.222. [12,000.]

Kent.

LELAND LEWIS DUNCAN, A calendar of wills relating to the county of Kent proved in the Prerogative court of Canterbury, between 1384 and 1559. Lewisham antiquarian society: Lee [printed] 1890. pp.[iii].v.93. [1600.]

W. E. BUCKLAND, The parish registers and records in the diocese of Rochester. Kent archæological society: Kent records [vol.i]: 1912. pp.xi.125. [500.]

Place Names

HENRY R. PLOMER, Index of wills and administrations now preserved in the Probate registry at Canterbury, 1396–1558 and 1640–1650. Kent archaeological society: Kent records (vol.vi): 1920. pp.viii.603. [30,000.]

LELAND L. DUNCAN, Index of wills proved in the Rochester consistory court between 1440 and 1561. Kent archæological society: Kent records (vol.ix): Canterbury 1924. pp.xii.234. [8000.]

Kent county, Del.

LEON DE VALINGER, Calendar of Kent county, Delaware, probate records, 1680–1800. Public archives commission: Dover 1944. pp.559.133. [5500.]

300 copies printed.

Lancashire.

[R. J. HARPER, JOHN CALEY and WILLIAM MINCHIN], Ducatus Lancastriæ. Pars prima. Calendarium inquisitionum post mortem, &c. temporibus regum Edw. I. . . . Car. I. Pars secunda. A calendar to the pleadings, &c. in the reigns of Hen. VII . . . Phil. & Mary. [Pars tertia. Calendar to pleadings, depositions, &c. in the

Place Names

reigns of Henry VII . . . Philip and Mary; and to the pleadings of the first thirteen years of the reign of queen Elizabeth. Pars quarta. Calendar to the pleadings from the fourteenth year to the end of the reign of queen Elizabeth.] [Commissioners on the public records:] 1823-1834. pp. [xi].391+[v].509+[v].644. [15,000.]

J[OHN] P[ARSONS] EARWAKER [1761-1800: W(IL-LIA)M FERGUSSON IRVINE; 1801-1810: R(ONALD) STEWART-BROWN], An index to the wills and inventories now preserved in the Court of probate, at Chester. Record society for the publication of original documents relating to Lancashire and Cheshire (vol.ii &c.).

 1545-1620 . . . (vol.ii): 1879. pp.xxxvi.224. [11,000.]
 1621-1650 . . . (vol.iv): 1881. pp.xii.303. [15,000.]
 1660 to 1680 . . . (vol.xv): 1887. pp.xii.380. [19,000.]
 1681 to 1700 . . . (vol.xviii): 1888. pp.x.365. [18,000.]
 1701 to 1720 . . . (vol.xx): 1889. pp.viii.261. [13,000.]
 1721 to 1740 . . . (vol.xxii): 1890. pp.viii.343. [17,000.]

Place Names

1741 to 1760 ... (vol.xxv): 1892. pp.viii.264. [13,000.]

1761 to 1780 ... (vols.xxxvii–xxxviii): 1898–1899. pp.[viii].200+[vi].123. [6000.]
> on the titlepage of vol.xxxviii the dates wrongly appear as 1741–1760.

1781 to 1790 ... (vol.xliv): 1902. pp.[vi].168. [8000.]

1791 to 1800 ... (vol.xlv): 1902. pp.[vii].242. [12,000.]

1801–1810 ... (vols.lxii–lxiii): 1911–1912. pp.viii.245+viii.201. [15,000.]

no records exist for the period 1651–1659.

HENRY FISHWICK, A list of the Lancashire wills proved within the archdeaconry of Richmond. Record society for the publication of original documents relating to Lancashire and Cheshire: (vol.x &c.).

1457–1680 ... (vol.x): 1884. pp.xii.324. [16,000.]

1681–1748 ... (vol.xiii): 1886. pp.vii.292. [15,000.]

1748–1792. Also a list of the wills proved in the peculiar of Halton, from A.D. 1615 to 1792 ... (vol.xxiii): 1891. pp.viii.144. [7000.]

Place Names

1793 to 1812. Also . . . in the peculiar of Halton . . . (vol.lxvi): 1913. pp.vii.106. [3000.]

1813–1837. . . . (vol.xc): 1947. pp.vi.153. [7500.]

1838 to 1858. To which is appended a list of Lancashire wills not recorded in the printed indexes . . . and which are now . . . in the Lancashire record office, from 1359 to 1858. Edited by Robert Dickinson . . . (vol.cv): 1953. pp.viii.165. [8000.]

R. D. RADCLIFFE, Schedule of deeds and documents, the property of colonel Thomas Richard Crosse . . . at Shaw hill, Chorley. Liverpool [printed] 1895. pp.83. [250.]

MARRIAGE bonds for the deaneries of Lonsdale, Kendale, Furness and Copeland [and Amounderness], part of the archdeaconry of Richmond, now preserved at Lancaster. Record society for the publication of original documents relating to Lancashire and Cheshire (vol.lxxiv &c.).

[i]. 1648–1710. Edited by John Brownbill . . . (vol.lxxiv): 1920. pp.viii.373. [3500.]

ii. 1711–1722. Edited by R[onald] Stewart Brown . . . (vol.lxxv): 1921. pp.[v].279. [3000.]

Place Names

    iii. 1723–1728. Edited by W[illia]m Fergusson Irvine ... (vol.lxxx): 1932. pp.[iv]. 278. [2500.]

    iv. 1729–1734 ... (vol lxxxi): 1932.pp.[iv]. 254. [2000.]

    v. 1734–1738 ... (vol.lxxxiii): 1933. pp.[iv]. 247. [2000.]

    vi. 1739–1745. Edited by Robert Dickinson ... (vol.c): 1949. pp.viii.243. [2000.]

W[ILLIA]M ASHETON TONGE, An index to the wills and administrations (including the 'infra' wills) now preserved in the probate registry at Chester for the years 1811–1820. Record society for the publication of original documents relating to Lancashire and Cheshire (vols.lxxviii–lxxix): 1928. pp.viii.328+viii.234. [22,500.]

MARRIAGE bonds of the ancient archdeaconry of Chester now preserved at Chester. Record society for the publication of original documents relating to Lancashire and Cheshire (vol.lxxxii &c.).

    i. 1700–1706–7. Edited by W[illia]m Asheton Tonge ... (vol.lxxxiii): 1933. pp.vi.302. [2000.]

    ii. 1707–1711. Edited by W[illiam] Fergusson Irvine ... (vol.lxxxv): 1935. pp.[iv]. 272. [2000.]

Place Names

    iii. 1711–1715 ... (vol.xcvii): 1942. pp.[iv].
285. [2000.]
    iv. 1716–1719. Edited by P. H. Lawson ...
(vol.ci): 1946. pp.[iv].333. [2500.]
in progress.

J. H. LUMBY, A calendar of the Norris deeds (Lancashire), 12th to 15th century. Record society for the publication of original documents relating to Lancashire and Cheshire (vol.xciii): 1939. pp.[vi].vii.287. [1171.]

Leek Wooton.

INDEX to the parish registers of Leek Wooton, co. Warwick, 1685–1742. 1887. ff.[i].7. [300.]
25 copies privately printed.

Leicester, city, county and diocese of.

C. V. KIRBY, Catalogue of the books, pamphlets, maps, views, mss., &c., relating to Leicestershire ... in the Central reference library. Public libraries: Leicester [1893]. pp.94. [1500.]

RETURN as to [on cover: custody of] parish documents ordered to be made by ... the Leicestershire county council. Leicester [printed] 1896. pp.14. [10,000.]

Place Names

HENRY HARTOPP, Calendars of wills and administrations relating to the county of Leicester. British record society: Index library (vol.xxvii): 1902. pp.xvi.314. [23,000.]

C. W. FOSTER, Leicestershire parish registers. Index to the bishops' transcripts in the registry of the archdeacon of Leicester, 1561 to 1700, embodying the Leicestershire transcripts in the registry of the bishop of Lincoln prior to 1700.... And also a list of Leicestershire parish registers prior to 1890: compiled by Henry Hartopp. Leicester 1909. pp.xi.52. [7500.]

HENRY HARTOPP, Leicestershire marriage licences. British record society: Index library (vol. xxxviii): 1910. pp.viii.542. [10,500.]

HENRY HARTOPP, Index to the wills and administrations proved and granted in the archdeaconry court of Leicester, 1660–1750. British record society: Index library (vol.li): 1920. pp. vii.391. [25,000.]

[A. BERNARD CLARKE], Leicestershire uncalendared wills 1489–1538. Leicestershire archeological society: Leicester [1951]. ff.[ii].35. [600.]*

LEICESTERSHIRE uncalendared wills, 1489–1538,

Place Names

with later items. Leicestershire archaeological society: Leicester [1952]. ff.35. [750.]*

HANDLIST of Leicestershire parish register transcripts. Museums and art gallery: Leicester 1953. pp.44. [10,000.]

Lincoln, city, county and diocese of.

A. GIBBONS, Lincoln marriage licences. An abstract of the allegation books preserved in the registry of the bishop of Lincoln, 1598–1628. 1888. pp.iii–viii.163. [3500.]

ERNEST L. GRANGE, A list of civil war tracts and broadsides relating to the county of Lincoln. Horncastle 1889. pp.[iii].20. [77.]
75 copies privately printed.

SOME unindexed wills at Lincoln [s.l. c.1890]. pp.4. [175.]
a list of wills, 1638–1640, found in the Bishop's registry.

[ALBERT GIBBONS], Wills and administrations in the court of the dean and chapter of Lincoln, 1534–1780. [Lincoln 1898]. pp.80. [3000.]
A–R only; no more published.

[ALBERT GIBBONS], Wills in the Consistory court

Place Names

of Lincoln. [Lincoln 1898]. pp.16. [650.]
covers 1501–1519 and A–Scryvener of 1520–1531; no more published.

C. W. FOSTER, Calendar of Lincoln wills ... 1320–1600[–1858]. British record society: Index library (vols.xxviii, xli, lii, lvii): 1902–1930. pp.xvii.349 + [ix].234 + [xi].410 + [xvii].501. [90,000.]

REGINALD C. DUDDING, Lincolnshire parish registers. Marriages. Index to vols.I–VI. 1916. pp.xii.247. [35,000.]
100 copies printed.

London, city, county and diocese of.

JOSEPH FOSTER, London marriage licences, 1521–1869. 1887. pp.xxiii. coll.1528. pp.1529–1595. [22,500.]

JOSEPH LEMUEL CHESTER and SIR GEO[RGE] J. ARMYTAGE, Allegations for marriage licences issued by the bishop of London, 1520 to 1610 [–1828]. Publications of the Harleian society (vols.xxv–xxvi): 1887–1888. pp.[iv].400+[iv].420. [13,500.]

REGINALD R. SHARPE, Calendar of wills proved and enrolled in the Court of husting, London,

Place Names

A.D. 1258–A.D. 1688, preserved among the archives of the corporation of the city of London. 1889–1890. pp.[v].xlviii.834+[iii].lv.924. [3000.]

REGINALD R. SHARPE, Calendar of coroners rolls of the city of London, A.D. 1300–1378. 1913. pp. xxviii.324. [300.]

REGINALD M[ORSHEAD] GLENCROSS, A calendar of the marriage licence allegations in the registry of the bishop of London. British record society: Index library (vol.lxii &c.).

    i. 1597–1648 ... (vol.lxii): 1937. pp.vii.436. [17,500.]

    ii. 1660–1700 ... (vol.lxvi): 1940. pp.vi.214. [7500.]

LONDON rate assessments and inhabitants lists in Guildhall library and the corporation of London records office. 1961. pp.[ii].50. [large number.]

PARISH registers. A handlist. Part 1: registers of church of England parishes within the city of London. Guildhall library: 1963. pp.[ii].70. [large number.]*

Lorraine.

VISCOUNT A. DE BIZEMONT, Bibliographie nobi-

Place Names

liaire de la Lorraine. Nancy 1897. pp.[iv].86. [363.]

Loudun.

J. X. CARRÉ DE BUSSEROLLE, Catalogue analytique d'aveux de fiefs rendus par des familles de la Touraine, de l'Anjou, du Maine et du Loudunois (XVIIᵉ et XVIIIᵉ siècles). Tours 1885. pp.[iii].214. [1500.]

Louisiana.

TITLE-LINE inventory of the parish archives of Louisiana. Work projects administration: Division of professional and service projects: Historical records survey: New Orleans [1939].*
loose-leaf.

Lyons.

[E. FAVIER], Tableau des registres paroissiaux de baptêmes, mariages et sépultures de la ville de Lyon conservés dans les archives municipales. Lyon 1889. pp.38. [1000.]

Maine, France.

J. X. CARRÉ DE BUSSEROLLE, Catalogue analy-

Place Names

tique d'aveux de fiefs rendus par des familles de la Touraine, de l'Anjou, du Maine et du Loudunois (XVIIe et XVIIIe siècles). Tours 1885. pp.[iii]. 214. [1500.]

Maryland.

JANE BALDWIN [*afterwards:* JANE BALDWIN COTTON; vols.iv–vii: and ROBERTA BOLLING HENRY], The Maryland calendar of wills. Baltimore.

 i. 1635–1685. 1901. pp.ix.219.lxii. [1100.]
 ii. 1685–1702. 1906. pp.[v].252.lxxv. [1000.]
 iii. 1703–1713. 1907. pp.[iii].258.lxxiii. [1000.]
 iv. 1713–1720. 1914. pp.[v].240.lxvi. [1000.]
 v. 1720–1726. 1917. pp.[ii].240.lxx. [1000.]
 vi. 1726–1732. 1920. pp.[ii].254.lxviii. [750.]
 vii. 1732–1738. 1925. pp.[iii].263.lxx. [1100.]
 viii. 1738–1743. 1918. pp.[iv].282.lxxxvi. [750.]

New Jersey.

CALENDAR of New Jersey wills, [administrations,] etc. New Jersey historical society: Documents relating to the colonial [, revolutionary and post-revolutionary] history of the state of New Jersey (1st ser., vol.xxiii&c.): Paterson, N.J. [&c.].

Place Names

i. 1670–1730. Edited ... by William Nelson. 1901. pp.lxxxix.662. [5000.]

ii. 1730–1750. Edited ... by A[braham] Van Doren Honeyman. 1918. pp.708. [5000.]

iii. 1751–1760. 1924. pp.469. [4000.]

iv. 1761–1770. 1928. pp.610. [5000.]

v. 1771–1780. Edited ... by E[lmer] T. Hutchinson. 1931. pp.747. [5000.]

vi. 1781–1785. 1939. pp.590. [4000.]

vii. 1786–1790. 1941. pp.337. [2000.]

viii. 1791–1795. 1942. pp.516. [4000.]

ix. 1796–1800. 1944. pp.581. [4000.]

Nicholas county.

ANNIE WALKER BURNS, Record of wills in Nicholas county, Kentucky. [Seat Pleasant, Md.] 1936. pp.[iii].86. [300.]*

Norfolk.

[T. R. TALLACK and FREDERIC JOHNSON], Marriages recorded in the register of the sacrist of the cathedral church of Norwich, 1697–1754. Norfolk and Norwich archaeological society: Norwich [1902]. pp.[iii].iv.143. [2000.]

M[ARGARET] A. FARROW, Index of wills proved

in the Consistory court of Norwich and now preserved in the District probate registry at Norwich, 1370–1550, and wills among the Norwich enrolled deeds, 1298–1508. Norfolk record society (vol.xvi): 1943–1945. pp.xiv.202+[iv]. 203–314+viii.315–448. [50,000.]

also issued as vol.lxix of the Index library.

M[ARGARET] A[RABELLA] FARROW and T[HOMAS] F[REDERICK] BARTON, Index of wills proved in the Consistory court of Norwich and now preserved in the District probate registry at Norwich, 1604–1686. Norfolk record society: Publications (vol. xxviii): Norwich 1958. pp.[vi].235. [10,000.]

Northamptonshire.

W[ILLIAM] P[HILLIMORE] W[ATTS] PHILLIMORE, A calendar of wills relating to the counties of Northampton and Rutland . . . 1510 to 1652. Index library (vol.i): 1888. pp.xvi.210. [15,000.]

Norwich.

WALTER RYE, Index to marriage licences, Consistory, Norwich, 1563–1588 from a mss. [*sic*] in the Public library. Norwich 1926. ff.[i].60. [2500.]*

INDEX to wills proved in the Consistory court

of Norwich. British record society: Index library (vol.lxix &c.).

 i. 1370–1550 and wills among the Norwich enrolled deeds, 1268–1508. Compiled and edited by M[argaret] A[nabella] Farrow. . . . (vol.lxix): 1945. pp.xiv.423. [20,000.]

 ii. 1550–1603. Compiled by M. A. Farrow. Edited by Percy Millican. . . . (vol.lxxiii): 1950. pp.188. [10,000.]

in progress; vol.ii was also issued as vol.xvi of the Norfolk record society publications, and vol.ii as vol.xxi.

Nottinghamshire.

CALENDAR of Nottinghamshire wills in the York registry, A.D. 1514 to 1619. Worksop 1890. pp.[ii].243. [13,500.]

THOMAS M[ATHEWS] BLAGG and F[REDERIC] ARTHUR WADSWORTH, Abstracts of Nottinghamshire marriage licences . . . 1577– . . . 1754[–1853]. British record society: Index library (vols.lviii, lx): 1930, 1935. pp.xiii.696+xi.751. [27,000.]

F[REDERIC] A[RTHUR] WADSWORTH and T[HOMAS] M[ATHEWS] BLAGG, A calendar of marriage licence bonds for the archdeaconry of Nottingham from 1754 to 1837. Part I. Thoroton society: Record

series (vol.x): [Nottingham] 1942. pp.112. [500.]
100 copies printed.

—— [another edition]. Abstracts of the bonds and allegations for marriage licences in the Archdeaconry court of Nottingham, 1754–1770. Transcribed . . . by T. M. Blagg. 1946–1947. pp.ix.285. [5000.]
150 copies printed.

Oxford.

J. S. W. GIBSON, Index to wills proved in the Peculiar court of the manor of Banbury, 1542–1858. Oxfordshire record society: Publications (vol.xl): Banbury 1959. pp.xv.128. [3000.]

Rutland.

W[ILLIAM] P[HILLIMORE] W[ATTS] PHILLIMORE, A calendar of wills relating to the counties of Northampton and Rutland . . . 1510 to 1652. Index library (vol.i): 1888. pp.xvi.210. [15,000.]

Salisbury, diocese of.

LIST (unofficial) of wills and administrations &c. (copies and originals) remaining at the diocesan registry, Salisbury. [*s.l.* 1928]. ff.[i].13. [400.]*

Place Names

[A SURVEY of the ecclesiastical archives of the diocese of Salisbury]. Pilgrim trust: Survey of ecclesiastical archives: [1952]. ff.23. [large number.]★

Sudbury.

W. BRUCE BANNERMAN and G. G. BRUCE BANNERMAN, Allegations for marriage licences in the archdeaconry of Sudbury, in the county of Suffolk, during the years 1684 to 1754[-1839]. Harleian society: Publications (vols.lxix–lxxii): 1918–1921. pp.viii.232+viii.458+viii.175+viii.330. [30,000.]

Suffolk.

FREDERICK ARTHUR CRISP, Calendar of wills at Ipswich, 1444–1600. 1895. pp.[vii].524. [20,000.]
100 copies privately printed.

[FREDERICK ARTHUR CRISP], Marriage licence bonds in the Suffolk archdeaconry registry at Ipswich, 1663–1750. 1900. pp.[v].241. [5000.]
100 copies privately printed.

MARRIAGE licences from the official note books of the archdeaconry of Suffolk deposited at the

Place Names

Ipswich probate court, 1613–1674. 1903. pp.[v]. 237. [5000.]

100 copies privately printed.

VINCENT B. REDSTONE, Calendar of pre-reformation wills, testaments, probates, administrations, registered at the Probate office, Bury St.Edmunds. Suffolk institute of archæology and national history: Proceedings (vol.xii [supplement]): Ipswich [printed] 1907. pp.xi.246. [6000.]

C. W. S. RANDALL CLOKE, A calendar of wills relating to the county of Suffolk proved in the Prerogative court of Canterbury between 1383 and 1604. [English monumental inscriptions society:] 1913. pp.[ii].95. [4000.]

100 copies printed.

WALLACE GANDY, Calendar of wills at Ipswich, 1751–1793. 1923. pp.[v].93. [4000.]

Surrey.

ALFRED RIDLEY BAX, Allegations for marriage licences issued by the Commissary court of Surrey between 1673–1770. Norwich 1907. pp.[ii].xi.870. [8500.]

[A. J. JEWERS *and others*], Surrey wills. (Archdeaconry court, Herringman register.) Surrey record society (vol.iv): [1915–]1920. pp.[iii].348. [1213.]

R. L. ATKINSON, Manuscript maps of Surrey: with a list of known examples in the Public record office. 1920. pp.8. [60.]

[A. V. PEATLING and CHARLES LETHBRIDGE KINGSFORD], Surrey wills. (Archdeaconry court, Spage register). Surrey record society (vol.v): 1921 [1922]. pp.[ii].xi.114. [329.]

Sussex.

WILLIAM HAMILTON HALL, Calendar of wills and administrations in the Archdeaconry court of Lewes... comprising... the whole of the eastern division of the county of Sussex. British record society: Index library (vol.xxiv): 1901. pp. and coll.xix.529. [25,000.]

EDWIN H. W. DUNKIN, Calendar of Sussex marriage licences. Sussex record society (vol.i &c.): Lewes [vol.(vi): Cambridge].
  [i]. Recorded in the Consistory court of the
     bishop of Chichester for the archdeaconry
     of Lewes, August, 1586, to March, 1642–3

Place Names

... (vol.i): 1902. pp.xvi.367. [3250.]

[ii]. — August, 1670, to March, 1728–9, and in the Peculiar court of the archbishop of Canterbury for the deanery of South Malling, May, 1620, to December, 1732 ... (vol.vi): 1907. pp.xvi.406. [7500.]

[iii]. Recorded in the Consistory court of the bishop of Chichester for the archdeaconry of Chichester, June, 1575, to December, 1730 ... (vol.ix): 1909. pp.xv.396. [5000.]

[iv]. Recorded in the peculiar courts of the dean of Chichester and of the archbishop of Canterbury. Deanery of Chichester, January, 1582–3, to December, 1730. Deaneries of Pagham and Tarring, January, 1579–80, to November, 1730 ... (vol.xii): 1911. pp.xv.303. [3000.]

[v]. Recorded in the Consistory court of the bishop of Chichester for the archdeaconry of Lewes, and in the Peculiar court of the archbishop of Canterbury for the deanery of South Malling, 1772–1837 ... (vols. xxv–xxvi): 1917–1919. pp.xvi.274+xv. 275–542. [6000.]

[vi]. Recorded in the Consistory court of the bishop of Chichester for the archdeaconry of Chichester, January, 1731, to December

Place Names

1774[-1800] ... (vols.xxxii, xxxv): 1926-1929. pp.xvii.276+ix.277-558. [7500.]

[JOHN E. RAY *and others*], Inventories of parochial documents: St. Peter's church, Bexhill, East Dean (near Eastbourne), Friston, Jevington, Ringmer, and Waldron. [*s.l.* 1915]. pp.10. [large number.]

F[REDERICK] W[ILLIAM] T[OWN] ATTREE, Notes of post mortem inquisitions taken in Sussex, 1 Henry VII. to 1649 and after. Sussex record society (vol.xiv): [Lewes] 1912. pp.xv.293. [1124.]

C. E. BARTLEY-DENNISS, Index to Penfold's m.s. Sussex pedigrees. [*s.l.*] 1930. ff.16. [750.]*

Tournai.

ADOLPHE HOCQUET, Archives de Tournai. Table alphabétique des testaments et des comptes de tutelle & d'exécution testamentaires. Société historique et archéologique de Tournai: Annales (new ser., vol.x, part 2): Tournai 1901. pp.197. [10,000.]

Utrecht.

R. VAN ROYEN, Beschrijving van de doop-, trouw-, begraafboeken, overlijdensregisters, enz. in de provincie Utrecht, dateerende van voor de invoering van den burgerlijken stand. 's-Gravenhage 1930. pp.151.

Place Names

Wellow.

CHARLES W. EMPSON. Index to the registers of baptisms, marriages, & burials of the parish of Wellow, in the counties of Southampton and Wiltshire. 1889. pp.[vii].284. [10,000.]

Worcester.

[SIR THOMAS PHILLIPPS], Index to wills at Worcester, 1492 to 1520[-1536]. [Middle hill *n.d.*]. pp.6+5-28. [3000.]

EDWARD ALEXANDER FRY, A calendar of wills and administrations preserved in the Consistory court of the bishop of Worcester. British record society and Worcestershire historical society.

    i. 1451-1600. [1899-]1904. pp.viii.480. [25,000.]
    ii. 1601-1652. 1907-1910. pp.[vii].257. [12,500.]

E. A. B. BARNARD, List of printed papers and miscellanea (with index); and of the pedigrees . . . in the Prattinton collections of Worcestershire history in the possession of the Society of antiquaries. [*s.l.*] 1932. ff.[ii].ii.162. [1500.]★

WORCESTERSHIRE parish registers of which copies exist in the library of the Society of genealogists [*s.l.* 1948]. pp.4. [50.]★

Place Names

York.

[F. COLLINS], Index to the Yorkshire wills proved in London during the time of the commonwealth (1649–60). Yorkshire archæological and topographical association: Record series (vol.i): Worksop [printed] 1885. pp.viii.49–300. [4500.]

[FRANCIS COLLINS and A. GIBBONS (1660–1688: ELY WILKINSON CROSSLEY)], Index of wills [administrations and probate acts] in the York registry. Yorkshire archæological and topographical association [archaeological society]: Record series (vol.iv &c.): [Huddersfield].

 1389–1514 . . . (vol.vi): 1889. pp.xii.204. [11,000.]
 1514–1553 . . . (vol.xi): 1891. pp.viii.246. [13,500.]
 1554–1568 . . . (vol.xiv): 1893. pp.[iii].212. [11,500.]
 1568–1585 . . . (vol.xix): 1895. pp.[ii].240. [13,000.]
 1585–1594 . . . (vol.xxii): 1897. pp.[ii].225. [12,500.]
 1594–1602 . . . (vol.xxiv): 1898. pp.[ii].206. [11,000.]
 1603–1611 . . . (vol.xxvi): 1899. pp.[ii].221. [12,000.]

Place Names

1612–1619 ... (vol.xxviii): 1900. pp.[ii].227. [12,500.]

1620–1627 ... (vol.xxxii): 1902. pp.[ii].183. [10,000.]

1627–1636. Administrations, A.D. 1627 to 1652 ... (vol.xxxv): 1905. pp.[iii].291. [16,000.]

1636–1652 ... (vol.iv): 1888. pp.vi.201. [11,000.]

1660–1665, and also of the unregistered wills and the probate acts, Aug. 1, 1633, to July 31, 1634, and of the 're infecta' wills, and the wills in bundles A and B ... (vol.xlix): 1913. pp.viii.166. [10,000.]

1666–1672, and also of the wills in certain peculiars ... (vol.lx): 1920. pp.vii.193. [11,500.]

1673–1680, and also of wills, etc. in the peculiar of Beeford together with tables of all printed indexes and of the principal collections of abstracts of Yorkshire wills, etc. ... (vol.lxviii): 1926. pp.viii.219. [8500.]

1681–1688, including the 'vacancies', June to August 1683, and April 1686 to December 1688 ... (vol.lxxxix): 1934. pp.xii.210. [10,000.]

Place Names

in progress?; the wills for 1653–1659 were proved in London.

INDEX of wills, etc., from the dean and chapter's court at York, A.D. 1321 to 1636; with appendix of original wills, A.D. 1524 to 1724. Yorkshire archæological society: Record series (vol.xxxviii): [Huddersfield] 1907. pp.[vi].96. [5000.]

[WILLIAM PAVER], Paver's marriage licences. Edited by John Wm. Clay. Yorkshire archæological society: Record series (vols.xl, xliii, xlvi): Worksop [printed] 1909–1912. pp.[iii].243+[iii].238+[iv].208. [15,000.]

covers the period 1630–1714; the earlier parts of William Paver's ms. appeared in the society's Journal, vols.viii, ix–xiv, xvi, xvii, xx and are indexed in:

A consolidated index to Paver's marriage licences (1567 to 1630), printed in the 'Yorkshire archæological journal'. Yorkshire archæological society: Extra series (vol.ii): Wakefield [printed] 1912. pp.[viii].152. [15,000.]

W. OLIVER, Index to the parish register transcripts belonging [to] the archdeaconry of Richmond ... from ... 1613 to 1848, now preserved in the Ripon diocesan registry, Leeds. Yorkshire parish register society: [Publications (vol.ci): Leeds] 1936. pp.xxii. [12,500.]

[J. CHARLESWORTH and ARTHUR V. HUDSON], Index of the wills and administrations entered in the registers of the archbishops at York, being consistory wills, &c., A.D. 1316 to A.D. 1822, known as the archbishops' wills. Yorkshire archæological society: Record series (vol.xciii): Wakefield [printed] 1937. pp.[v].97. [4000.]

Zuidholland.

H. BROUWER, Beschrijving van doop-, trouw- en begraafboeken, benevens van de registers van overledenen enz. in Zuid-Holland, dateerende van vóór de invoering van den burgerlijken stand. 's-Gravenhage 1929. pp.315.

Zwolle.

J. WIJNBEEK, Overzicht der doop-, trouw- en doodboeken, berustende in het oud-archief der gemeente Zwolle. [Zwolle 1901]. pp.34.

Ref
Z
5311
B47